# THE BENCH
AND BAR

SPY
Leslie Ward
(1851–1922)

# THE BENCH AND BAR

## GREAT LEGAL CARICATURES
### FROM *Vanity Fair* BY *Spy*

Morris L. Cohen

HUGH LAUTER LEVIN ASSOCIATES, INC.

# ACKNOWLEDGMENTS

There are a few fine collections of *Vanity Fair* caricatures still in private hands. One of these, owned by John A. Franks, LL.M., London solicitor and member of the Law Society, is the source of the illustrations in this volume. We express our gratitude to Mr. Franks for making his collection available for this purpose and for sharing his vast knowledge of *Vanity Fair* and of Sir Leslie Ward with us. Needless to say, Mr. Franks is in no way responsible for any shortcomings or errors in this work. Mr. Franks began collecting in 1950 and has acquired a number of the original *Vanity Fair* caricatures, as well as most volumes of the magazine and albums, and some of the related ephemera. He is a collector of taste, tenacity, understanding, and—most important—generosity and openness.

Miss Sara Waterson, picture researcher of London and Suffolk, England, gave invaluable help in locating the caricatures and facilitating and supervising their photography. We are grateful for her experience and knowledge in working with graphic materials, and in expediting a somewhat complicated project.

David Ratzan and Eryn Simmers, Yale undergraduates, were indispensable assistants in completing this book. Mr. Ratzan worked extensively with coordination of the images and biographies and offered original interpretive ideas. Ms. Simmers handled the technical production expertly and was a calming and organizing force throughout. They have my gratitude.

Thanks are also due to the scholars who have worked so well and so long with these materials. Their publications have provided guidance and valuable information to relative novices like myself. The writers whom I found particularly helpful include Jerold J. Savory, Roy T. Matthews and Peter Mellini, and Eileen Harris. Their publications are listed, with other useful sources, in the bibliography at the end of this volume.

Finally, thanks to my patient publisher and to his indefatigable staff—particularly Ellin Silberblatt and James Muschett.

Morris L. Cohen
New Haven
September 5, 1996

FRONTISPIECE: *Leslie Ward.* PAL. *Vanity Fair,* Nov. 23, 1889.

# CONTENTS

# FOREWORD

As a young lawyer in 1950 browsing through an old bookshop, I came across an album of coloured *Vanity Fair* caricatures. I paid two pounds and was hooked.

The series of *Vanity Fair* albums provides a unique record of Society over the forty-five years they were produced. Collectors of legal and political material from this period can find in the albums fascinating and relevant examples. Lawyers, specifically, are very well served. Now Professor Morris Cohen has made the fascinating selection of Spy's caricatures of lawyers of the bench and bar, reproduced here in their pristine colours.

I can understand only too well how a bibliophile such as Professor Cohen could have been drawn to this archive and then draw from it for the benefit of others. How could an eminent and distinguished librarian such as Professor Cohen pass up the opportunity to share with others this feast for eye and mind? He is providing an unique panoply to which otherwise there is no easy access. It is true that many lawyers have one or more of these curious sketches, some of which have been hung on office walls here or there over the last hundred years, but often these have lost some of the vibrancy of colour that the images in this book now display. Others may be more fortunate with the present state of their prints, but they may not have the biographic notes that add to their appreciation.

Spy and his fellow artists worked in a special mode. After all, this was the age of the Impressionists. In its own way, *Vanity Fair* was very much a part of that artistic movement, reacting to the then-new era of portrait photography. This is addressed in the prefaces of the first two *Vanity Fair* albums:

"A photograph which gives every feature with absolute correctness may yet fail to convey the distinct idea of character at which the artist and the writer have alike aimed in these sketches,"[1] and "In the portraits the object has been to give the brutal truth, in the notices to deal out the bare yet sufficient justice, with the object in both cases of leaving as exact an impression of the man as can be arrived at."[2]

I add a health warning for those who previously have not been exposed to the *Vanity Fair* experience, and which itself is an expression of my appreciation of this work by Professor Cohen. This selection may be highly addictive.

I believe this is a book that the reader will truly enjoy.

John A. Franks, LL.M.
London
October 2, 1996

Notes on the Foreword:
1 *Vanity Fair Album*, 1870, preface
2 *Vanity Fair Album*, 1880, preface

# INTRODUCTION

This volume brings together two elements in the history of English caricature that produced a genre noteworthy as an art form, as satire, and as social history. These elements are the English weekly magazine *Vanity Fair* and the work of the artist Leslie Ward, who, under the pen name Spy, drew over thirteen hundred caricatures for *Vanity Fair*. These two forces combined to represent a high point in English satire's traditional focus on judges and lawyers, or the bench and the bar.

## Vanity Fair

*Vanity Fair, a Weekly Show of Political, Social and Literary Wares*, was founded by Thomas Gibson Bowles in 1868 with an investment of £200, half of that sum having been borrowed from friends. Bowles edited and published it as a politically conservative but lively society magazine until 1889, when he sought a more personal involvement in politics. He then sold the magazine for £20,000. *Vanity Fair* continued with gradually declining success under new ownership and a succession of editors until 1914, when it was merged into *Hearth and Home*, which, as its name suggests, was a very different magazine.

Bowles (1842–1922) was born out of wedlock but raised by his father, Thomas Milner Gibson, a wealthy and well-connected politician and Member of Parliament. Little is known about Bowles's mother, Susan Bowles, but the infant Thomas was accepted into Gibson's family and cared for by Gibson's wife along with her own children. Bowles grew up privileged, traveled in France, studied at King's College, London, and briefly held a minor government post in taxation. He pursued literary interests, which included writing regularly for the daily *Morning Post* and contributing to several society magazines. He acquired a varied group of colorful and influential friends who, with others like them, became both the subjects of his new magazine and the core of its audience.

Bowles was twenty-six when he started *Vanity Fair*, the venture being a logical extension of his life at that point. He chose the title and the magazine's motto, "We buy the truth," from John Bunyan's allegorical novel *Pilgrim's Progress*. The first issue continued and enlarged that focus of a metaphorical marketplace: "In this show, it is purposed to display the vanities of the week, without ignoring or disguising the fact that they are vanities, but keeping always in mind that in the buying and selling of them there is to be made a profit of truth." William Makepeace Thackeray's popular satirical novel *Vanity Fair* was undoubtedly another influence.

After a somewhat shaky start, *Vanity Fair* became a success and made many innovations in English popular literature, including the caricatures that are the focus of this book. The weekly magazine contained news of world events and articles on politics and the arts, but its emphasis was on society news and personalities. Regular features also included literary and theater reviews, fashion news, games, travel articles, and fiction in varied formats. Even more than its later counterparts, such the American *Vanity Fair*, *The New Yorker*, and *Punch*, it was written for the social elite, the upper classes of Victorian and Edwardian England. Its contents and its advertisements were geared to high society, although it attracted a broader audience. While Bowles incurred the animosity of the royal family and other victims of his wit, he remained a popular figure in society. Mention in his magazine was much sought after, and gossip flowed in steadily from well-connected informants.

In its third month of publication, in the issue of January 23, 1869, Bowles announced that the next issue would contain "a full-page cartoon of an entirely novel character printed in chrome-lithography." Thus was born the series of caricatures that was to ensure the success of *Vanity Fair* and much of its importance in English popular culture and social history. The issue of January 30, 1869, included a brilliant caricature of Benjamin Disraeli signed Singe, the pen name of Carlo Pellegrini, an Italian artist who was a popular figure in London's artistic and society circles. Under the name Ape (the English translation of Singe), Pellegrini became *Vanity Fair's* primary caricaturist until he was succeeded by Leslie Ward.[1] Disraeli had recently resigned his first tenure as prime minister and was Bowles's favorite in the political struggle with William Gladstone, whose caricature by Pellegrini appeared the very next week. These initial illustrations have become classics of political caricature, and many consider that the early work of Pellegrini set a standard for the magazine. The role of the caricatures in the success of *Vanity Fair* can be seen from their impact on the magazine's circulation. Only 619 copies of the first issue were sold. Sales dropped to 408 for the second issue. One month after the caricatures were introduced sales shot up to 2,529 copies.[2]

The drawings of Disraeli and Gladstone were each accompanied by a biographical sketch of the subject written by Bowles and signed Jehu Junior. The editor's admiration for Disraeli and dislike of Gladstone were apparent in these sketches. Such biographical essays, usually done with the same satire as the caricatures, became a regular feature of *Vanity Fair*. They were written by Bowles as long as he was editor and signed with the Jehu Junior pseudonym, which referred to one or both of two biblical characters named Jehu who lived successively in the ninth century B.C.E.[3] The biographical pieces have not had the sustained popularity of the caricatures. Their wit and succinct phrasing, however, offer some of the best satire in Victorian prose. All of the sketches that accompanied the caricatures in this book are set out in full in the second section of this volume.

Among the choicer thrusts to be found in the essays that accompanied Spy's legal caricatures are the following:

*But his manners are imperfect. He has often been rude to counsel; he delights to say nasty things of and to solicitors; and he frightens witnesses. His voice grates, and his manner repels. He has a long upper lip which he is able to wreathe with an unpleasant curl.* (Sir Edward Ebenezer Kay, p. 114)

*He is a great pulveriser of frivolous defences; but he is a very deaf Judge, and often tries people in more ways than one.* (Mr. Justice William Ventris Field, p. 114)

*He was a very skillful, a very vivacious, and a very witty advocate; but he is now less vivacious, and his wit has entirely evaporated, though he still often says things that are laughed at because it is supposed that they are intended to be laughed at. . . . He is an upright, sensible, and magnificently ugly man.* (Sir John Charles Frederick Sigimund Day, p. 115)

*An Irishman by race, brogue, and humour, Mr. Pope was born so long ago that the event has by common consent been forgotten. . . . Mr. Pope has the ordinary culture and manners of the Bar; he is much experienced in*

*Parliamentary practice, and greatly given to showing his experience by digging up old cases; he has a rich, vulgar, effective humour; and he is good-tempered and persuasive.* (Samuel Pope, p. 113)

The weekly caricatures were a major element in the success of *Vanity Fair*, and the high quality of their reproduction was a large factor in their appeal. Lithography, invented in 1798, was already widely used before *Vanity Fair*, as was chromolithography, a form of color printing that was based on lithography. However, further technical advances in the transfer process and in the paper used to transfer the images occurred about the time that *Vanity Fair* was founded. Bowles used the lithography firm that owned the processes and plates of George Baxter, a pioneer in color printing, and which employed Baxter's son, also a talented color lithographer. This assured Bowles the highest quality of color printing for the caricatures.4

With the success of the caricatures, Bowles started a companion publication, *The* VANITY FAIR *Album: A Show of Sovereigns, Statesmen, Judges, and Men of the Day; With Biographical and Critical Notices*. The albums offered annually a collection of the caricatures and accompanying biographical sketches from the previous year's issues of *Vanity Fair*. In his preface to the first album for 1869 (published in 1870), Bowles (signed, as usual, Jehu Junior) described his rationale for the caricatures and sketches:

*The object of the caricature portraits and the accompanying notices to be found in this volume is to give that more complete idea of our rulers which it is both desirable, and, indeed, necessary to possess in order to be able to form a just conception of their acts and objects. The portraits speak for themselves. The result of close study from actual life, they have been drawn in no unkindly spirit, but with the sole object of so presenting the essential characteristics found in the subject as to bring them home forcibly to all whom they would otherwise escape. The same may be said of the notices by which the portraits are supplemented and completed. Whatever else these may be, they are honest; they have been written with the single object of telling the exact truth; and although there are many allusions which will only be understood by those who are behind the scenes, I have endeavoured in each case to give of every man an idea clear in itself, and sufficient to warrant safe inferences as to the position he holds in, and the course he is likely to take upon, public affairs.*

Bowles's rich life after he sold *Vanity Fair* in 1889 gives ample evidence of his wide-ranging abilities. His biography in the *Dictionary of National Biography* (1922–1930 Supplement, pp. 98–99) devotes only one sentence out of over thirty to his involvement with *Vanity Fair*. He had a long and active political career that included several periods in the House of Commons. He was an experienced sailor and, although not formally trained in law, was an authority on admiralty and international law. He also continued *The Lady*, a magazine for women that he had started in 1885. Bowles died in 1922 while on holiday in Spain. A full account of his life can be seen in Leonard Naylor's lively biography.5

**Leslie Ward and the Spy Caricatures**
Although Pellegrini was the primary caricaturist for *Vanity Fair* from 1869 to 1875, several others shared those duties. During 1874 and 1875, however, Pellegrini provided virtually

every weekly drawing, completing the astonishing number of 107 caricatures in two years. Perhaps as the result of burnout following that period, he temporarily gave up this work for portrait painting at the urging of his friend James Whistler. Pellegrini was less successful at this, however, and soon returned to drawing for *Vanity Fair*, but not on the same scale as in earlier years. He contributed approximately 160 caricatures from July 1877 until his death in January 1889. Many artists and critics, including Max Beerbohm, considered Ape to have been the finest of the *Vanity Fair* caricaturists, but he never achieved the wide fame and popularity of his successor, Leslie Ward.6

In 1873, when Bowles was looking for additional artists to help produce the weekly drawings, he was introduced to the twenty-two-year-old Leslie Ward by a mutual friend, the artist John Everett Millais. Bowles was shown some of Ward's drawings, was immediately impressed, and hired him. Ward's first drawing, "Old Bones," a caricature of the zoologist Dr. Richard Owen, appeared on March 1, 1873. He was a regular contributor during the next forty years, and over thirteen hundred of his caricatures were published in *Vanity Fair*. That represented more than half the total of approximately twenty-five hundred that appeared during the life of the magazine, and an even greater proportion of the legal caricatures.

Leslie Ward was born in 1851 and was descended from artists on both his father's and mother's sides. His father, Edward Matthew Ward, was a historical painter, and his mother, Henrietta Ward, was a respected portrait painter in her own right. Henrietta Ward's father and grandfather were each distinguished engravers and artists, and she also had an uncle and great-uncle who were well-known painters. During his youth, Ward's home was frequented by outstanding artists, writers, actors, and society figures—the perfect environment for a future *Vanity Fair* artist. In fact, Ward often sketched and caricatured not only visitors to his parents' home but also fellow students at Eton and at the schools of the Royal Academy where he studied.

In his rather bland autobiography, *Forty Years of "Spy,"* Ward describes the qualities of a good caricaturist:

*The caricaturist, I am convinced, is born, not made. The facility which comes to some artists after long practice does not necessarily avail in this branch of art; for the power to see a caricature is in the eye of a beholder, and no amount of forcing the perceptions will produce the point of view of a genuine caricaturist. A good memory, an eye for detail, and a mind to appreciate and grasp the whole atmosphere and peculiarity of the "subject," are of course essentials... together, very decidedly, with a sense of humour.7*

In that same book, Ward explains how he chose the pen name Spy. At their initial meeting, Bowles rejected Ward's first suggestion and handed him a copy of Dr. Johnson's dictionary to find another name. Ward describes opening the book to the letter *S*, where his eye fell on the word *spy*:

*"How's that?" I said. "The verb to spy, to observe secretly, or to discover at a distance or in concealment."*

*"Just the thing," said Bowles. And so we settled it.8*

That anecdote and other references in his autobiography point up a difference in technique between Ward and Pellegrini.9 While Ape occasionally worked from formal sittings, Ward more often would seek out his "victims" in the field, sketch them at work or play, and then revise and complete the sketch back in the studio. This was particularly effective with lawyers and judges, whose courtroom appearances provided full opportunity for Ward to observe and sketch them in their professional settings. When a caricature of Ward himself appeared in *Vanity Fair* (see the frontispiece to this book),[10] the accompanying biographical sketch included the following comments on his stalking:

> *He is a keen sportsman whose quarry is man; and he could tell stories of stalking which would make the most hardened deer-stalker pale with envy. The methods which he has employed, the ruses which he has adopted, the characters which he has assumed, the deceptions which he has practised, the plots which he has hatched, or which he has had hatched for him, would fill a volume; for there are but few men who are so unartificial as to voluntarily offer their portraits for* Vanity Fair. *Most of them must be studied unawares, in order that their counterfeit presentments may be true presentments of them as they really are, and not the graceful presentments which are compassed by sitters in a studio where Nature is consciously or unconsciously superseded by the airs and affectations of Art.*[11]

Ward had great success with his caricatures of lawyers and judges, and they have remained his most popular work. They undoubtedly benefited from Ward's familiarity with the law courts and his extensive friendships with members of the legal profession.[12] It is worth noting that both Bowles and Ward had been parties in lawsuits during their lives.

Ward did over seventy drawings of judges and over ninety of lawyers (including both barristers and solicitors, and a few from Ireland, Scotland, France, and some Commonwealth countries). One hundred of Spy's caricatures are reproduced here, the largest number to have been published together in a book. The portraits represent all segments of the judiciary, from the highest courts of appeal to the lowest magistrates and peace officers. They include a few individuals who, though trained in the law, were not primarily known for their practice as barristers or solicitors. These include several Members of Parliament, other government officials, and writers such as Sir Anthony Hope (Hawkins), author of *The Prisoner of Zenda.*

Looking at some of Ward's first caricatures, then, we find the same qualities that David Low and other great caricaturists saw in Pellegrini's work, whether it be in the shrewd and thoughtful Justice Mellor (p. 11), contemplating the proceedings from his bench while absentmindedly sucking on his little finger, or in the whimsical Sir Robert Lush (p. 12), disarmingly elfish but calculating behind the opaque lenses of his eyeglasses.[13] Ward was often to achieve this same success in his later work in the law courts, most notably in the caricatures of Lord Halsbury (p. 52), Justice Channell (p. 76), Justice Bruce (p. 84), Justice Cozens-Hardy (p. 85), and Sir Joseph Walton (p. 90). What is most effective in these particular caricatures is not so much the obvious features but the direct, and seemingly unavoidable, incarnation of their personalities in their physical appearances.

Yet as Sir Leslie Ward moved through his career we find fewer of this type of caricature and more examples of what he liked to call the "characteristic portrait."[14] Ward also considered himself an expert portrait painter, and, not surprisingly, he often found that some of his subjects were more amenable to portraiture than strict caricature. A trend toward a more objective, realistic representation becomes apparent in his work, especially in his later years at *Vanity Fair.* As early as 1885, with the drawing of Sir Edward Gibson (p. 30), we find the beginnings of this trend, as the subject strikes a pose reminiscent of many portraits, his right hand tucked into his coat, while the sketch itself reveals little of the personality of the depicted individual. By the turn of the century, the trend toward portraiture, although not universal, becomes more apparent, as evidenced in Ward's caricatures of Mr. Arthur Newton (p. 60), Lord Advocate Murray (p. 69), Mr. Edward Hall (p. 93), Sir Edward Edgcumbe (p. 107), and Mr. Hemmerde (p. 110).[15] These "characteristic portraits" convey something of a subject's temperament and personality, but without the effort to summarize the entire person in one revealing moment, and they lack the satirical edge of caricature that Ward achieved elsewhere. In their extreme form, some of these later portraits were criticized as being little more than fashion illustrations. However, these are not the drawings that have achieved lasting popularity.

Around the turn of the century, after Bowles had departed from *Vanity Fair*, changes were also apparent in the biographical notices accompanying the caricatures. Before 1900, most of the biographies were much more like the best caricatures—verbal attempts to capture the man and the moment succinctly by highlighting a few details, rather than the standard linear narrative that one expects of a biography. As such, these short pieces by Jehu Junior were properly *sketches,* and they employed one or the other of two distinct stylistic methods. The first was to focus on a central trait that expressed the essence of the subject, with the rest of the information about him hanging off this central theme almost parenthetically. Often such a sketch ended with a witty one-line epigram that tied the whole sketch together. Good examples of biographies of this type are of the meticulous Mellish (p. 112) and the slow and steady Bruce (p. 122). In the second approach, the biographer felt that his subject could not be reduced to a single overarching character trait, but must be conveyed in the totality of his persona. In such cases, Jehu Junior fired off a staccato of sharp, independent phrases, which, although seemingly unconnected, gave one a good overall picture of the man, as in the sketch of Ebenezer Kay (p. 114). In the early period, there was often also a highly conscious political bias written into many of the sketches, so that after reading them, one knew Jehu Junior's opinions on Gladstone, Radicalism, Toryism, and Home Rule. These sketches as a group revealed an active engagement in the politics of the day.

After 1900 the quality and integrity of the sketches decline. Increasingly, the measured and careful prose of the earlier time yields to longer, ever more rambling narratives of the subjects' lives. Jehu abandons his seat of judgment for the more mundane role of chronicler and raconteur. For the first time we see the introduction of anecdotes, which diffuse the attempt to understand a single personality by adding another person to the picture (for example, see those on Jelf, p. 123, and Asquith, p. 124). Now, instead of focusing on the characteristic or main accomplishment that made the man interesting, there is only an unqualified list of his doings; rather than praising his major strengths or lampooning his weaknesses in the law courts, there is more attention paid to his ability to entertain in society and putt on the links. Finally, instead of reverence for the integrity and majesty of the law, there is often an unbecoming fascination with the subject's ability to earn fantastic sums.

The individuals from this period decrease in importance, and at one point Jehu apologizes for the relative obscurity of his subject. He changed from the biographer who reserved the right to pronounce judgment on the men and policies of his day—a prophet with the authority of God, or a king who gives ample warning before destroying his enemies—to the Jehu who merely recounts the actions of his subjects. No longer a celebration of the bench and bar, these sketches are reduced to mere gossip or descriptions of little interest and less wit. Perhaps this growing blandness can be attributed in part to the growth of libel actions and their increasing success. Although no actions were brought against Bowles for comments in *Vanity Fair* until 1881,[16] one was brought that year. It ended inconclusively as far as Bowles was concerned, and apparently he actually lost only one such action.[17]

Despite the later decline of Spy's satirical touch, his legal caricatures have remained among the most popular images of the English legal profession. They are rivaled in popularity only by Daumier's *Law and Justice* prints, although they are in a much different genre artistically. Reproductions of Ward's drawings continue to decorate the offices, societies, and schools of the legal profession, particularly in America. The collecting of Spy prints is still pursued by some, although the pictures have become increasingly rare and very expensive. Bound volumes of *Vanity Fair* and the annual albums are almost unobtainable, and the competition for individual prints is very keen. Few libraries have substantial holdings, and only a handful have a complete run of the volumes.

In addition to the prints themselves and the few books that have reproduced them selectively, there have been several other forms of reproduction. Cigarette trading cards bearing *Vanity Fair* caricatures were popular at one time, and there have been attempts to produce ceramic figures of *Vanity Fair* caricatures along with plates and bowls bearing such illustrations. These are all now very rare, and information about them is difficult to obtain. Shown here is a cigarette card with the Spy caricature of Anthony Hope (Hawkins), the barrister who wrote *The Prisoner of Zenda*. The full caricature can be seen on page 65.

Ward was knighted in 1918 and died in London on May 15, 1922, the same year in which Bowles died. His work can be viewed within the English tradition of satire directed at the law. All of the major figures in English satirical art gave special attention to the law and its characters.[18] This history includes the work of William Hogarth (1697–1764), Thomas Rowlandson (1756–1827), James Gillray (1757–1815), Isaac Cruikshank (1765–1811), and his sons Isaac Robert (1789–1856) and George Cruikshank (1792–1878).

Some of the same negative qualities of lawyers and judges that were featured in the work of those masters of English satire are suggested in Leslie Ward's caricatures—pomposity, cunning, disdain, and coldness. By and large, however, Ward's drawings are milder than those of his predecessors. Less apparent in *Vanity Fair* are the greed, corruption, and plain silliness that are commonplace in eighteenth-century satire of the legal profession.

What gave Ward's caricatures their wide and continuing popularity? There are many factors: the large number of drawings he executed, allowing the winnowing process to

**WILLS'S CIGARETTES**

"ANTHONY HOPE."
"Vanity Fair," 2nd. Series No. 20.

leave many of merit surviving; the artistic quality of most of his work; the excellence of the color printing; the humor and satire in the best of the caricatures; and the authenticity of detail resulting from Ward's power of observation and familiarity with his subjects and their milieu. Perhaps equally significant is his ability to reveal recognizable traits of personality and character, particularly as represented among lawyers and judges, irrespective of place and time.

One of the most balanced views of Ward's work has been given by Roy T. Matthews, a leading scholar of *Vanity Fair*. In his article "Spy," Matthews describes the critical views of Max Beerbohm, David Low, and others. He then emphasizes Ward's positive contributions:

*From both historical and personal influences Ward's caricatures are symbolic of the refined joviality and good-natured humour of many Victorians and representative of his family, education and private life. His innate artistic ability and his talent were shaped and moulded by the attitudes and values of that society with which he so closely identified. Because of his rank in the English social system and his personal predilections, he never attempted to alienate himself from his class. Consequently, his critics argue, Ward's works have been judged in a manner less favourable than those caricatures by artists who made a conscious effort to separate themselves from their milieu and their subjects. Yet, a case can be argued that Ward, by being closer to the values of his day than other caricaturists, was more accurate in catching the flavour and tone of his times.[19]*

Thus the art of both the man and that of the magazine gain integrity and stature by remaining part of the society they portrayed.

JUDGES THE CLAIMANT
The Honourable Sir John Mellor
(1809–1887)
May 24, 1873
*Judges* 7

A Little Lush
The Honourable Sir Robert Lush
(1807–1881)
May 31, 1873
*Judges* 8

THE TICHBORNE CASE
Mr. Henry Hawkins, Q.C.
Baron Brampton
(1817–1907)
June 21, 1873
*Men of the Day* 64

SCOTCH LAW
Duncan McNeill
Lord Colonsay and Oronsay
(1793–1874)
September 13, 1873
*Statesmen* 154

THE CLAIMANT'S COUNSEL
Dr. Edward Vaughan Hyde Kenealy
(1819–1880)
November 1, 1873
*Men of the Day* 71

A LAWYER
Serjeant John Humffreys Parry
(1816–1880)
December 13, 1873
*Men of the Day* 73

THE EXCHEQUER
The Honourable Sir George William Wilshere Bramwell
Baron Bramwell
(1808–1892)
January 29, 1876
*Judges* 11

FORMERLY OF THE CARLTON
The Honourable Sir Anthony Cleasby
(1804–1879)
February 5, 1876
*Judges* 12

APPEALS
The Right Honourable Sir George Mellish, D.C.L.
(1814–1877)
December 30, 1876
*Judges* 13

ATTORNEY-GENERAL
Sir John Holker
(1828–1882)
February 9, 1878
*Statesmen* 265

THE LAW
The Right Honourable Sir George Jessel
(1824–1883)
March 1, 1879
*Men of the Day* 195

THE NEW JUDGE
The Honourable Mr. Justice Douglas Straight
(1844–1914)
May 10, 1879
*Men of the Day* 199

CITY JUSTICE
Alderman Sir Robert Walter Carden, Knt., M.P.
(1801–1888)
December 11, 1880
*Statesmen* 348

THE SOLICITOR-GENERAL
Sir Farrer Herschell, M.P., Q.C.
(1837–1899)
March 19, 1881
*Statesmen* 353

A LORD OF APPEAL
The Right Honourable Lord Colin Blackburn
(1813–1896)
November 19, 1881
*Statesmen* 381

DODO
The Honourable Sir Adolphus Frederick Octavius Liddell, K.C.B., Q.C.
(1846–1920)
September 30, 1882
*Men of the Day 263*

THE CLERK OF THE PARLIAMENTS
Sir William Rose, K.C.B.
(1808–1885)
February 14, 1885
*Men of the Day* 326

THE CRIMINAL CODE
The Honourable Sir James Fitzjames Stephen, K.C.S.I.
(1829–1894)
March 7, 1885
*Judges* 14

THE UMPIRE
The Honourable Sir Joseph William Chitty
(1828–1899)
March 28, 1885
*Judges* 15

DUBLIN UNIVERSITY
The Right Honourable Edward Gibson, P.C., Q.C., LL.D.
Baron Ashbourne
(1837–1913)
July 4, 1885

*Statesmen 466*

JUMBO
Mr. Samuel Pope, Q.C.
(1826–1901)
December 12, 1885
*Men of the Day* 346

BOW STREET
Sir James Taylor Ingham, M.A., Knt.
(1805–1890)
February 20, 1886
*Men of the Day* 353

THE LORD ADVOCATE
The Right Honourable John Blair Balfour, P.C., M.P.
Baron Kinross of Glasclune
(1837–1905)
May 1, 1886
*Statesmen* 489

THE SERJEANT
Sir John Simon, Knt., M.P., Serjeant-at-Law
(1818–1897)
September 25, 1886
*Statesmen 500*

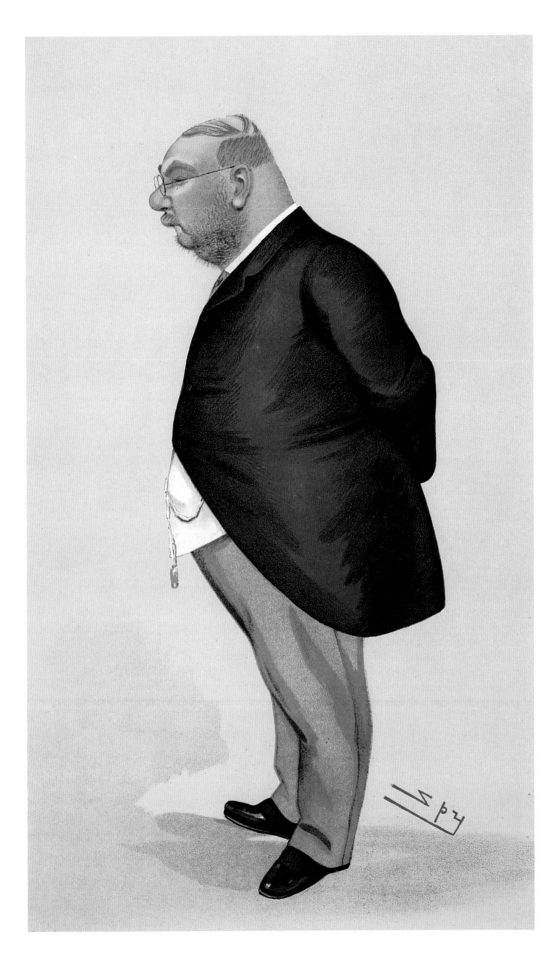

MUNICIPAL CORPORATIONS
Sir Albert Kay Rollit, Knt., LL.D., M.P.
(1842–1923)
October 9, 1886
*Statesmen* 502

STAY, PLEASE
Mr. Justice William Ventris Field
Baron Field of Bakeham
(1813–1907)
April 30, 1887
*Judges* 18

COURT ROLL
Mr. Charles Isaac Elton, Q.C., M.P.
(1839–1900)
August 6, 1887
*Statesmen* 525

YORK
Mr. Frank Lockwood, Q.C., M.P.
(1846–1897)
August 20, 1887
*Statesmen* 526

THE HOME SECRETARY
The Right Honourable Henry Matthews, Q.C., M.P.
Viscount Llandaff
(1826–1913)
September 10, 1887
*Statesmen 527*

COSTS DISALLOWED
The Honourable Sir Edward Ebenezer Kay
(1822–1897)
January 7, 1888
*Judges* 20

THE NEW JUDGE
The Honourable Sir Arthur Charles
(1839–1921)
February 4, 1888
*Men of the Day* 395

THE GREAT UNMARRIER
The Right Honourable Sir James Hannen, Knt., P.C.
Baron Hannen
(1821–1894)
April 21, 1888
*Judges* 21

GUILELESS
The Right Honourable Lord Justice Henry Cotton
(1821–1892)
May 19, 1888
*Judges* 22

2ND COMMISSIONER
The Honourable Sir John Charles Frederick Sigimund Day
(1826–1908)
October 27, 1888
*Judges 23*

3RD COMMISSIONER
The Honourable Sir Archibald Levin Smith
(1836–1901)
November 23, 1888
*Judges* 24

BELLS
The Right Honourable Lord Edward Beckett (Denison) Grimthorpe, Q.C., LL.D.
Baron Grimthorpe
(1816–1905)
February 2, 1889
*Statesmen* 559

WORKINGHAM
Sir George Russell, M.P., D.L.
(1828–1898)
March 2, 1889
*Statesmen 563*

FOR THE 'TIMES'
Mr. John Patrick Murphy, Q.C.
(1831–1907)
May 4, 1889
*Men of the Day* 423

HE DEFENDED ARABI
Mr. Alexander Meyrick Broadley
(1847–1916)
December 14, 1889
*Men of the Day 452*

MR. JUSTICE GRANTHAM
The Honourable Sir William Grantham
(1835–1911)
March 15, 1890
*Judges* 28

BOW STREET
Mr. James Vaughan
(1814–1906)
October 25, 1890
*Men of the Day* 487

FROM THE OLD BAILEY
Sir Hardinge Stanley Giffard
Earl of Halsbury
(1823–1921)
November 8, 1890
*Statesmen* 575

CHIEF MAGISTRATE
Sir John Bridge
(1824–1900)
April 25, 1891
*Men of the Day* 505

UNDER SHERIFF
Mr. Thomas Beard
(1828–1895)
May 23, 1891
*Men of the Day* 509

LONDON SESSIONS
Sir Peter Henry Edlin, Q.C., J.P., D.L.
(1819–1903)
October 31, 1891
*Judges* 34

HE CAN MARSHALL EVIDENCE
Mr. Charles Willie Mathews
(1850–1920)
February 6, 1892
*Men of the Day* 531

JUDICIAL POLITENESS
The Right Honourable Sir Charles Synge Christopher Bowen, P.C., D.C.L., LL.D., F.R.S.
Baron Bowen
(1835–1894)
March 12, 1892
*Judges* 36

ADMIRALTY JURISDICTION
The Honourable Sir John Gorell Barnes
Baron Gorell
(1848–1914)
February 18, 1893
*Judges* 39

HE HAS WRITTEN ON COMPANIES
Sir Henry Thring
Baron Thring
(1818–1907)
June 29, 1893
*Statesmen* 614

THE MARLBOROUGH STREET SOLICITOR
Mr. Arthur John Edward Newton
(1860–1907)
September 21, 1893
*Men of the Day* 574

THAT WON'T DO, YOU KNOW
The Honourable Sir Lewis William Cave
(1832–1897)
December 7, 1893
*Judges* 42

OUR WEAKEST JUDGE
The Honourable Sir William Rann Kennedy
(1846–1915)
December 14, 1893
*Judges* 43

A HASTY JUDGE
The Honourable Sir Arthur Kekewich
(1832–1907)
January 24, 1895
*Judges* 44

HE SUCCEEDED LORD BLACKBURN
Sir Edward Macnaghten, P.C.
Baron Macnaghten
(1830–1913)
October 31, 1895
*Statesmen 660*

ANTHONY HOPE
Mr. Anthony Hope Hawkins
(1863–1933)
December 26, 1895
*Men of the Day* 640

COMMERCIAL COURT
Mr. Justice James Charles Mathew
(1830–1908)
March 12, 1896
*Judges* 45

BENEVOLENCE ON THE BENCH
The Honourable Sir Alfred Wills
(1828–1912)
June 25, 1896
*Judges* 46

DIVORCE COURT
Mr. Frederic Andrew Inderwick, Q.C.
(1836–1904)
July 30, 1896
*Men of the Day* 654

LORD ADVOCATE
Mr. Andrew Graham Murray
(1849–1942)
October 22, 1896
*Statesmen* 680

EQUITY
The Honourable Sir James Stirling
(1836–1916)
January 28, 1897
*Judges* 47

LONG LAWRANCE
The Honourable Sir John Compton Lawrance
(1832–1912)
March 18, 1897
*Judges* 48

His Father Invented Pickwick
Mr. Henry Fielding Dickens, Q.C.
(1849–1933)
May 13, 1897
*Men of the Day* 681

A Judicial Joker
The Honourable Francis Henry Bacon
(b. 1832)
November 4, 1897
*Judges* 50

NORTH EAST BETHNAL GREEN
Sir Mancherjee Merwanjee Bhownaggree, K.C.I.E., M.P.
(1851–1933)
November 18, 1897
*Statesmen* 691

WE SHALL SEE
Mr. Justice John Charles Bigham
Viscount Mersey
(1840–1929)
February 3, 1898
*Judges* 51

AN AMIABLE JUDGE
The Honourable Mr. Justice Sir Arthur Moseley Channell
(1838–1928)
February 17, 1898
*Judges* 52

A SPORTING LAWYER
Sir John George Witt, Q.C.
(1837–1906)
March 17, 1898
*Men of the Day* 708

DANKY
Mr. William Otto Adolph Julius Danckwerts
(1853–1914)
June 23, 1898
*Men of the Day 716*

BARGRAVE
Mr. Henry Bargrave Finnelly Deane, Q.C.
(1846–1919)
August 4, 1898
*Men of the Day* 721

A Judicial Churchman
The Honourable Sir Walter George Frank Phillimore, Bart., D.C.L.
Baron Phillimore
(1845–1929)
November 24, 1898

*Judges* 53

HE BELIEVES IN THE POLICE
Mr. Franklin Lushington
(1823–1907)
August 17, 1899
*Men of the Day* 757

COMPANY LAW
Mr. Justice Henry Burton Buckley
(1845–1935)
April 5, 1900
*Judges* 55

DICK
Lord Chief Justice Richard Everard Webster
Viscount Alverstone
(1842–1915)
November 1, 1900
*Judges* 57

SLOW AND STEADY
Mr. Justice Gainsford Bruce
(1834–1912)
December 6, 1900
*Judges* 60

FAIR, IF NOT BEAUTIFUL
The Honourable Mr. Justice Cozens-Hardy
Baron Cozens-Hardy
(1838–1920)
January 24, 1901
*Judges* 61

A BLUNT LORD JUSTICE
Lord Justice John Rigby
(1834–1903)
March 28, 1901
*Judges* 62

BOSEY
Sir Frederick Albert Bosanquet, Common Law Serjeant of London
(1837–1923)
November 21, 1901
*Judges* 63

SOUTH DONEGAL
Mr. John Gordon Swift MacNeill, K.C., M.P.
(1849–1926)
March 13, 1902
*Statesmen* 748

VICAR GENERAL
Mr. Charles Alfred Cripps, K.C., M.P.
(1852–1941)
April 10, 1902
*Statesmen* 750

A LAWYER ON THE BENCH
The Honourable Sir Joseph Walton
(1845–1910)
July 24, 1902
*Judges* 66

SIR EDWARD
Sir Edward George Clarke, K.C.
(1841–1931)
June 11, 1903
*Men of the Day 882*

A Scots Lawyer
Alexander Burns Shand, P.C., D.C.L., LL.D.
Baron Shand
(1828–1904)
July 23, 1903
*Judges* 61

SOUTHPORT DIVISION
Mr. Edward Marshall Hall, K.C., M.P.
(1858–1929)
September 24, 1903
*Statesmen* 759

ULSTERMAN K.C.
Mr. Robert Alfred McCall, K.C.
(1849–1934)
November 19, 1903
*Men of the Day* 900

RUFUS
Mr. Rufus Daniel Isaacs, K.C.
Marquess of Reading
(1860–1935)
February 18, 1904
*Men of the Day* 908

ERMINED URBANITY
The Honourable Sir Arthur Richard Jelf, K.C.
(1837–1917)
May 19, 1904
*Judges 62*

SLIM
Sir Horace Edmund Avory, K.C.
(1851–1935)
June 2, 1904
*Men of the Day* 918

BRAINS
The Right Honourable Herbert Henry Asquith, M.P.
Earl of Oxford and Asquith
(1852–1928)
July 14, 1904
*Statesmen* 769

THE PRESIDENT OF THE LAW SOCIETY
Mr. Thomas Rawle
(1842–1916)
July 6, 1905
*Men of the Day* 971

Bow Street
Mr. Robert Henry Bullock-Marsham, R.H.
(1833–1913)
October 12, 1905
*Men of the Day* 985

SO VALUABLE AN ADVOCATE SHOULD BECOME A SUCCESSFUL PARLIAMENTARIAN
Lord Robert Cecil, K.C., M.P.
(b. 1864)
February 22, 1906
*Men of the Day* 1003

A Man of Law and Broad Acres
Mr. Justice Sir Reginald More Bray
(1842–1923)
October 17, 1906
*Men of the Day* 1036

A Successful First Speech: 'Moab is my Washpot'
Mr. Frederick Edwin Smith, M.P.
Earl of Birkenhead
(1872–1930)
January 16, 1907
*Men of the Day* 1049

WORSHIP STREET
Mr. H. Chartres Biron
(1863–1940)
March 27, 1907
*Men of the Day* 1059

JUDICIAL LIGHT WEIGHT
The Honourable Mr. Justice Charles John Darling
Baron Darling
(1849–1936)
May 8, 1907
*Men of the Day* 1065

NORTH LONDON
Mr. Edward Snow Fordham
(1858–1917)
January 15, 1908
*Men of the Day* 1102

SMALL FREEHOLDS
Sir Edward Robert Pearce Edgcumbe, LL.D., D.L., J.P.
(1851–1929)
February 5, 1908
*Men of the Day* 1105

S A M
Sir Samuel Thomas Evans, K.C., J.P.
(1859–1918)
February 12, 1908
*Men of the Day* 1106

THE SILVER VOICED
Lord Bernard John Seymour Coleridge
Baron Coleridge
(1851–1927)
January 13, 1909
*Men of the Day* 1154

THE NEW RECORDER
Mr. Edward G. Hemmerde, K.C.
(1871–1948)
May 19, 1909
*Men of the Day* 1172

**The Hon. Sir John Mellor**
(1809–1887) Page 11
A steady, smooth-going lawyer's life has been Mr. Justice Mellor's. He was called to the Bar, became a Q.C. Recorder of Warwick, unsuccessful candidate for Warwick, Recorder of Leicester, Member of Parliament for Yarmouth, Member for Nottingham, and so at last a Justice of the Queen's Bench with a Knight's Patenet, all in less than thirty years. As an advocate he was not brilliant, but he was a safe adviser, extremely well-bred, and polite without condescension even to his clients when he came into contact with them. His opinion of a case was almost as good as the judgement of the Court, and he never shrank from advising a compromise rather than fight out a weak cause. At Nisi Prius he was quiet and gentlemanly; he never bullied a witness or lost his temper with one, whom he always endeavoured rather to persuade of the weakness of his opponent than of his own strength. In Banco he was wont however to trouble the Court by sticking to his argument heedless of queries or suggestions from the Bench; and his argument was always a good one, for he has read and digested more both of Common Law and of Equity doctrine than is usual. But he was formed by Nature to sit on the Bench himself. It is not the least of the proofs he has given of his fitness for the position he occupies that he now keeps aloof from all public affairs save those which concern his office, and that he never does or says anything to draw attention to his personality. He judges the Claimant as he judges all his cases with unwearied patience and impartiality, and his attitude has been throughout in strict consonance with that unimpassioned dignity which should always be felt most when passions are excited as they are over this trial. If I were the victim of an unjust accusation likely to need an interminable investigation I should wish no better than to be tried by Mr. Justice Mellor; if I were an astute criminal hoping for an escape from the fatigue of the Bench I should fear no worse.

**The Hon. Sir Robert Lush**
(1807–1881) Page 12
Good-natured, good-humoured, and ever equally ready to attempt a joke himself or to enjoy it when made by others is Mr. Justice Lush. When told that the mess-toast had been changed from "Women and Wine" to "Lush and Shea," he wisely and modestly said, "A spell of sobriety will do the Bar no harm," and "a little Lush may do the Bench some good." The Bar indeed remarked that the more highly-flavoured witticisms were distasteful to him, and reproached him with being a good fellow put in to play the part of a heavy Father. His oratory was usually of a humdrum kind, yet he was often amusing, and he had a knack of gaining the confidence of hostile witnesses which made him a dangerous adversary. As a Judge he is so just and so conscientiously laborious that it is often almost painful to hear him striving to enlighten and inform obtuse jurymen, and it has been remarked of him that he leaves nothing to the jury but to say Amen to him or else to proclaim themselves fools. He is sixty-six years of age, he lives in St. John's Wood, and his motto is "Virtute non astutia."

**Mr. Henry Hawkins, Q.C.**
**Baron Brampton**
(1817–1907) Page 13
During the thirty years that he has been an advocate, Mr. Hawkins has made for himself as such a first-rate reputation. He is not an orator in the high-flown sense, and it was commonly supposed that he did not know how to deal with a hostile witness until his cross-examination of Mr. Baigent became famous. He was declared also not to work at his briefs, until his masterly and most proper summary of the Tichborne case brought him into favourable comparison with Sir John Coleridge, and proved that he had spent his days and nights over an overwhelming mass of evidence. Yet it has always been found that he had a knack of winning verdicts against the heaviest odds. He is very quick at seeing the weakness of his opponent, quicker perhaps than in marshalling his own forces, and when before the enemy has often been known to attempt fine strokes in generalship. Withal he has the drollest and most irresistible manner, and the hoarsest voice extant, which latter gift of nature he is once said to have declared was worth £5000 a-year to him; and when he undertakes to tickle a witness, to talk at a doubtful juror, or even to out-manoeuvre the sacred Bench itself, it is not without chances of success and the certainty of making a good retreat in case of failure. With these qualities he has naturally been engaged in some of the greatest trials that have been held of late years—so the cases of Roupell, of Strahan Paul and Bates, of the Sun Fire Office, and of Saurin V. Starr are all associated with his name. He once was fond of horse-racing and of the fair sex; but he has long ceased to study the minor prophets, and merely rides now for the sake of health, on a horse well known to the early frequenters of Rotten Row; while he has proved, when sitting in the Crown Court, that he can be as serious as any occasion demands. Being as he is an undeniably well-read and sound lawyer, and having been now long in the front rank of his profession, it has been a matter of surprise to many that he has not been made a Judge, all the more that the fact of his picking his briefs proves him to be rich enough to enjoy that luxury were it offered to him. Possibly one reason may be that he has never secured the opportunity of serving any Party in Parliament, for although he offered himself to the electors of Barnstaple eight years ago, he was defeated, and has not since tempted Providence in that way.

**Duncan McNeill**
**Lord Colonsay and Oronsay**
(1793–1874) Page 14
For a young Scotchman who has set his hopes across the Border there is no more promising profession than the Law, and there is none in which Scotchmen have gained so disproportionate a share of prizes. Wherefore presumably it was that John McNeill sent his boy Duncan to the working University of St. Andrew's, and then to the Scottish Bar. This was nigh upon sixty years ago and Duncan, now a hale old gentleman of over eighty, has passed since then through every kind of official post until he arrived at last safely in the haven of the House of Lords. He has been successively Sheriff of Perthshire, Solicitor-General for Scotland, Lord Advocate, Dean of the Faculty of Advocates, a Lord of Session, and finally Lord Justice-General and President of the Court of Session, until upon his retirement he was permanently installed upon the red benches. He is one of the old Conservatives who believed in Peel, and he still continues a member of Carlton while many of his former friends have crossed to the Reform. He fitly represents the Majesty of Scotch Law, invested with the Mercy of a British Peerage.

**Dr. Edward Vaughan Hyde Kenealy**
(1819–1880) Page 15
A year ago the name of Kenealy was scarcely known save to a few discerning solicitors. Even among them it had but little weight, for it was that of an Irishman, of a struggling barrister, of one to be trusted perhaps some day with an important brief, but not so far by any means in the first flight of advocates or with any chance of coming into it. In truth he was a strange man as times go, a somewhat sickly yet quick, eager, impetuous man, furnished with many qualities notable indeed, but dangerous. A man rather to insist fiercely on a principle or an argument than to get on the soft side of judge or jury, not therefore as it appeared a man to win verdicts. Neither was he believed to be at all fully versed in the letter of the law. He seemed indeed to be penetrated with its spirit, for against its violation he had protested as the unlistened to will protest, in writings of a fiercely discontented character. In 1863 he had published a volume of verses filled with anger and manifestly the result of reading "Faust," and those he had dedicated to Mr. Disraeli, whom he declared to be superior to Pitt inasmuch as Pitt had not written "Vivian Grey" or "Sybil." The following year he had published other verses which he had "most respectfully inscribed" to Chief Justice Cockburn, declaring that he felt a "fervent admiration, honour and regard" for "that judge, jurist, and scholar." Both sets of verses were indifferent, bad, and neither of them took the world by storm. So that Kenealy of Castle O'Kenealy seemed destined to pass an unregarded life and to consume if anything only himself with the fire that burnt within him.

An opportunity however at length arose not unsuitable to the exhibition of the powers which he felt himself to possess. The Claimant of the Tichborne Name and Estates had seen himself nonsuited and his fortunes reduced to the lowest ebb. Committed for trial on a charge of perjury, a bankrupt and without money, his cause had been successively abandoned by many lawyers; and in this extremity it was that Dr. Kenealy came forward and took it up. Whether by his conduct of it he had improved his professional prospects may by the Bar be questioned; that he has by it made himself famous and formidable is undoubted. Seldom has there been seen in these latter days such audacity as he has displayed, and the pugnacity with which he has encountered and stood up to such potent personages as Editors, Jurymen, and Judges—including even the Chief Justice of his fervent admiration—has been a scandal to many and a marvel to all. He handles a friendly witness cleverly yet it is remarkable that he is not very successful in cross-examination, for he seems to delight in meeting hostility in any shape. His language is not highly polished but it is uncommonly strong, his impressive utterance is calculated to persuade his hearers that he is earnest and sincere in his convictions, and though small in stature his voice is big enough to be that of a giant. Withal he is in himself and for himself highly sensitive and has about him a certain sadness and dejection such as are not unseldom found in men of excitable temperament. He was educated at Trinity College, Dublin, he is so great a linguist as to have mastered no less than a dozen languages, and in one of them at least is capable of saying in plain terms what others would scarcely dare to hint. Also he is the one recorded man who has ruffled the temper of Mr. Hawkins.

**Serjeant John Humffreys Parry**
(1816–1880) Page 16
An unsuccessful barrister rich only in a knowledge of Welsh literature can hardly make a handsome provision for his children. Wherefore, and possibly also from a doubt whether he had the capacity to achieve distinction in any other career, John Humffreys Parry was sent by his father at an early age into the office of a City merchant, there to cast up totals and docket letters. But the young man thought himself made for other than these base uses, and, having as he thought a power of speech, joined a debating society, where, showing much readiness in words and a notable talent for recasting the whole system of Society, he was pronounced to be a great orator. Upon this he procured a small appointment in the British Museum and began to read for the Bar, to which he was called at the somewhat late age of seven-and-twenty. And he soon showed that the Debating Society had been right in their estimate of him. His oratory indeed was and still is rather of the stumping kind, he is a believer in action so far as to impart it even to his wig by the skin of his forehead, he drapes himself in his gown with the movement of a Senator of Melodrama, and his perorations have a boldness of flight which a confirmed Ranter might envy. With these antecedents and talents it was natural that he should soon present himself as a Candidate for Parliament. He did so at Norwich in 1847 and again at Finsbury in 1857, on both occasions as a Radical of the redder kind—only to suffer on both occasions a signal defeat. Since then Serjeant Parry has not been heard of at Public Meetings, possibly because he has become less desirous to upset an established order of things into which he has now adopted himself. For he has great abilities, and by them has raised himself in his Profession to be quite one of its successful men, so that his is a name which gains much favour with Solicitors and gives much confidence to clients. He is one of the leaders of the Home Circuit and

earns an income large enough to make any man a Conservative.

### The Hon. Sir George William Wilshere Bramwell
### Baron Bramwell
(1808–1892) Page 17

The son of a banking clerk who had been taken into partnership by his firm, Mr. Bramwell was instructed in such things as it is necessary for a commercial young man to know. But he had a spirit above dealing only with other people's money, and at one-and-twenty he went abroad to seek his fortune. Not finding it, he returned to England, took to law, and at thirty was called to the Bar. With dogged pertinacity he plodded at his work, and though no orator, he was soon known as a trustworthy counsel, doing his very best for his clients, though never bolstering up a bad case by twisting the facts or confusing the law. He always won the ear of the Court, for his reputation was that of a highly continent and moral man; yet he was of neither University; he had never been in Parliament, and to this day is so little of a politician that no man knows his Party creed. He did not seem, therefore, marked out for distinction, but in 1851 he "took silk," and as a leader achieved great success, being especially without a rival as a case-lawyer. Only five years later he was made a Judge, and he has done signal honour to the choice made of him. He is often severe in his sentences, yet he always subordinates his judicial *dicta* to judicial principles, and he is especially ready at testing analogies and in curbing the adventurous dexterities of the Bar. A right-minded, plain man of eight-and-sixty is Baron Bramwell, known sometimes to the profane as "Taffy," only once accused in ribald mess-verse of an amorous adventure, yet genial, full of good sense, and twice married.

### The Hon. Sir Anthony Cleasby
(1804–1879) Page 18

Birched at Eton, educated at Cambridge, Third Wrangler of his year, afterwards a Fellow of Trinity, and late of the Carlton, Sir Anthony Cleasby has been from the first one of the most intensely respectable of advocates. For thirty years after he was called to the Bar he wore a stuff gown, and when at last he took silk he was not held for a successful leader. But being a staunch Conservative, with much contempt for all the delusions of Liberalism, he had early begun to contest seats in Parliament; and when a vacancy on the Bench became disposable seven years ago, it was remembered that he had served his Party by getting three times defeated at great expense. Upon this he was made a Baron of the Exchequer, where he has shown, with much anxiety to be impartial, the result upon the mind of forty years of advocacy, and occasionally a certain brusque and dictatorial manner, besides some disposition to direct juries in matters of fact. He is popular in Society, being a pleasant talker.

### The Rt. Hon. Sir George Mellish, D.C.L.
(1814–1877) Page 19

Sixty-two years ago the Dean of Hereford had a son and sent him to the Bar. The young man went the Northern Circuit and made steady progress, so that in 1861 he was made a Queen's Counsel, and in 1870 received the appointment of a Lord Justice of Appeals, together with knighthood, and the titular right to advise Her Majesty in a Council which is never assembled. He has, indeed, some shining judicial qualities. Some judges make and some mar the law; Lord Justice Mellish does neither. He never analyses the construction of a judicial decision, nor ventures on the erection of a doctrine, but he avoids the fault of founding his judgements on a single case. Favoured whether by his memory or by his study of the reports, he can usually lay a ready hand on several cases on all fours with that under consideration. He is, moreover, so courteous as to have been named indifferently "the Chesterfield of the Bench," and "the milk of human kindness." He never discloses bias in a case until he gives his decision, he attaches great importance to the arguments against him, and he is not uncommonly found to speak in one way and to decide in the other. He is a very favourable specimen of a "fusion" judge, since he combines exact knowledge of the doctrines of considerable Equity with a knowledge of the principles of the Common Law. He is withal much bound by precedent, and is held therefore to be eminently safe. As to his personal merit there never has been any question, for he has many warmly attached friends, who are all thoroughly convinced of it, and whom he confirms in their conviction by much good-natured geniality.

### Sir John Holker
(1828–1882) Page 20

Unlike most of his fellow-lawyers in Parliament, Sir John Holker began politics comparatively early in life, being already a Member of the House of Commons at the boyish age of four-and-forty. He is a North-countryman, and he made the most of considerable powers and a handsome gift of speech, so that the Conservative chiefs, who have been poorly off for lawyers, made him in two years Solicitor-General and shortly afterwards Attorney-General. He has worked his way up manfully, and filled his official positions with much credit and comfort, being a shrewd man and reliable for his law. Although only fifty years of age, he has been articled to a solicitor and twice married.

### The Rt. Hon. Sir George Jessel
(1824–1883) Page 21

Mr. Zachariah Jessel, a diamond merchant, of Savile Row, was blessed five-and-fifty years ago with a son. This son he sent to University College, London, and thence to the Bar. The young man was very industrious and very able; he soon mastered the whole of the law of Real Estate; he became well known as a successful pleader; he was made a Queen's Counsel and a Bencher of his Inn; and in 1871, while yet under fifty, he was appointed Solicitor-General by Mr. Gladstone. In 1873 he was still further elevated by being appointed Master of the Rolls; and in 1875 he became a Judge of the Supreme Court of Judicature, being the first Jew ever appointed to the Judicial Bench in England. He is what is called a strong Judge; he conducts his business in the most admirable manner and with the most perfect taste; and he is not only very learned in the law, but very sound and very just in his decisions. Personally he is very popular, much admired, and greatly respected; and he owes all he is, and nearly all he has, to his own great natural talents, untiring industry, and undoubted honesty.

### The Hon. Mr. Justice Douglas Straight
(1844–1914) Page 22

Douglas Straight was born four-and-thirty years ago. In 1865 he was called to the Bar, and five years later he was elected Member of Parliament for Shrewsbury, and regaled with an election petition against his return. He never took any notable part in public affairs, but devoted himself to his private business as a lawyer, and in this he had considerable success. His practise lay chiefly at the Old Bailey, but was varied by cases of other than the purely criminal kind; and he has acted for some time as junior counsel for the Treasury. Mr. Straight has dabbled considerably in journalism; he has worked very hard and energetically, and has got on well both with men and women; so that he is much known in various walks of life. He has now been appointed Puisne Judge of the High Court of the North-West Provinces of India, and his elevation has given much satisfaction to all the friends of the new Judge.

### Alderman Sir Robert Walter Carden, Knt., M.P.
(1801–1888) Page 23

Seventy-nine years ago there was born Robert Carden. He went into and out of a regiment of foot. He went into stockbroking. He went into some City Company, and being a Sheriff when the Queen visited the City, was knighted. He became Lord Mayor. He became a Conservative. He fought many electioneering fights at great costs and charges, and at last got elected to the Commons House for Gloucester and then for Barnstaple. He is a grandson of the original John Walter, who so ably conducted the *Times*, and he is believed to have a share in it at the present time. He sits often on the Bench and administers City justice. He is a very well-meaning old gentleman.

### Sir Farrer Herschell, M.P., Q.C.
(1837–1899) Page 24

The worthy Dissenting minister of Gloucester-place would have been pleased had he lived to see his son as he is now. Born forty-four years ago, Farrer Herschell was educated at University College—where afterwards he became Examiner in Common Law—and at Bonn on the Rhine. He was called to the Bar in 1860, and received silk in 1872; but even then few discerned in him the germs of greatness; and when in 1873 he was Recorder of Carlisle many considered he had reached his zenith. But a profound belief in yourself and unflagging industry are powerful weapons, and when the funereal "Shillibeer" took to politics and was elected for Durham as a Liberal success was assured. In Parliament he was useful in attack; and if he has scarcely succeeded in office, he is always listened to with the respect due to a law officer of the Crown, and to one of that Semitic race that must ultimately rule over the land.

He has had, or seemed to have, but one hobby—the abolition of breach of promise cases; he is not afflicted with originality or genius; he has the capability of making good friends and few enemies; and is as proud of his own success as if he had not deserved it.

### The Rt. Hon. Lord Colin Blackburn
(1813–1896) Page 25

Colin Blackburn was born eight-and-sixty years ago, passed through Eton, distinguished himself at Cambridge, and went to the Bar. Here he soon became known for a dry vein of Scotch humour, and for a great capacity for work. He was known to be a staunch Conservative, yet he was regarded as being so good a lawyer that a Liberal Ministry made him a judge. He proved a keen and upright judge, and in 1876 a Conservative Government made him a Lord of Appeal in Ordinary and a Judge of the Supreme Court of Judicature. With this he became a limited Peer, entitled to sit and vote with the Lords as long as he holds office. His title is not hereditary; but he is an old bachelor.

### The Hon. Sir Adolphus Frederick Octavius Liddell, K.C.B., Q.C.
(1846–1920) Page 26

Born four-and-sixty years ago a younger son of the first Lord Ravensworth, and early endowed with that name of "dodo" which has remained with him through life, Sir Adolphus betook himself to the Bar. In the course of time he became so far successful at the Bar as to leave it for the Home Office, where he has been Permanent Under-Secretary and the real dispenser of hanging and pardoning for many years.

He is an extremely kindly, amiable man, full of geniality, and most popular with all who know him. Withal he works hard and conscientiously, and is a very valuable public servant.

### Sir William Rose, K.C.B.
(1808–1885) Page 27

The fortunes of the Rose family were made by Lord Thurlow, who recommended to William Pitt the original George Rose—a son of Lord Marchmont's—who served the Ministry and the State with industry and ability in Parliament, dispensed patronage, acquired property, and founded an official family. The present Sir William is the grandson of George, and the brother of Lord Strathnairn. He is the third of his family who has held the office of Clerk of the Parliaments, and is a Tory of the best old type, with all the courtliness, amenity, and true-heartedness of the Grandison school.

Born seven-and-seventy years ago, he was at forty appointed Deputy-Clerk, and thirty years later blossomed into Clerk of the Parliaments, a post he still illustrates. Those who know him least would imagine that they only know a man of perfect social accomplishments. Those who know him best know him as an official of the greatest zeal in the conduct of his important public duties, and as a chief who governs his subordinates with the potent sway which belongs to a man who rules by the force of his own example and by the irresistible touch of sympathetic feeling; while those who have ventured to break a lance with him have learnt the existence of a stubborn force which never fails to be evoked when any question arises concerning those matters upon which he is the great authority—namely, the practise, the dignity, and the traditions of the House of Lords.

### The Hon. Sir James Fitzjames Stephen, K.C.S.I.
(1829–1894) Page 28

The eldest son of the Right Honourable Sir James Stephen, who was a Cambridge Professor and an Under Secretary of State, was born six-and-fifty years ago. After going through Eton, and King's College, London, he graduated as a B.A. at Trinity College, Cambridge; was called to the Bar, and graced the Midland Circuit with his company; afterwards becoming Recorder of Newark-on-Trent, and being prominently employed in a big ecclesiastical case. Being rising and ambitious, he proclaimed himself a Liberal, and in 1865 essayed to represent Harwich in Parliament, with the result of being placed last out of the four on the poll, with only seventy-seven votes. In 1868 he took silk, and at the end of the following year was appointed a Legal Member of the Council of the Viceroy of India, in which torrid dependency he remained until he had effected, for its special benefit, a high-class Code of Criminal Procedure. When he came back from India he again proclaimed himself a Liberal, and essayed to represent Dundee, with the same result of being placed last out of the four candidates. Later on he drafted a Criminal Code for this country too, which Sir John Holker introduced to Parliament in 1878, without getting it attended to; but he was appointed one out of four most learned Commissioners who next year produced a most learned report on that same Draft Code. Since then the House of Commons has not condescended to trouble itself much about such trifling details. But Sir James's labours have brought their reward. In 1875 the Inns of Court made him a Professor of Common Law; in 1877 he was nominated a K.C.S.I.; and in 1879 he was elevated to the Bench as a Judge of the Queen's Bench Division of the High Court of Justice. He is also a D.C.L. of Oxford, and an LL.B. of London. He is a very able man indeed, very learned and very sound, and one of the great lights of the Bench; is the author of well-known works on the Law of Evidence and on Criminal Law; and in the latter branch of legal knowledge his supremacy is quite unquestioned. He has also published in the *Nineteenth Century* his opinion that we could live very well without religion. In the trial of causes, he looks tremendous when his moral indignation rises. He once wrote for the *Saturday Review*.

### The Hon. Sir Joseph William Chitty
(1828–1899) Page 29

Ever since these isles were peopled, some Chitty or other has been always writing or editing books about English Law. The present Judge of this distinguished name is not the offspring of Chitty's Statutes or of Chitty on Contracts, but of Chitty's Archbold—that is to say, he is the second son of the late Mr. Thomas Chitty, who was a very eminent and popular Special Pleader in his day.

Born seven-and-fifty years ago, young Joseph William was sent to Eton to do sums and learn his Latin grammar; and then, having proceeded to Balliol College, Oxford, by the aid of diligence and good ability he took a First Class in Classics in 1851, afterwards being elected a Fellow of Exeter, and becoming Vinerian Scholar in 1852. Of course he next went in for Law; in 1856 was called to the Bar at Lincoln's Inn (of which he was made a Bencher nineteen years later), took silk in 1874, grew to be the Leader in the Rolls Court, and carried on an enormous practise. Strange to say, he omitted to pose as a legal author. Presently he drifted into politics, and in 1880 he sat as a Liberal M.P. for corrupt Oxford, in which posture he might possibly have remained, had he not, in September, 1881, been appointed Judge of the Chancery Division in the room of Sir George Jessel, who was moved on to the Court of Appeal.

Like his father, Sir Joseph has always been a favorite with his fellow-men; and, being of a robust frame, he from time to time distinguished himself in various athletic exercises. He rowed for his University, he took much interest in the Inns of Court Volunteers (of which he was a Major), and for many years he officiated as the Umpire at the Oxford and Cambridge Boat-Race. When raised to the dignity of the Bench, however, he put away umpiring and lawn-tennis and similar childish things. In Court

he is agreeable, although his voice is very penetrating; but business progresses rather slowly there—they say because he wants to talk quite as much as the counsel appearing before him; wherefore they irreverently call him "Mr. Justice Chatty." The son of a lawyer, he married the daughter of a Judge.

### The Rt. Hon. Edward Gibson, P.C., Q.C., LL.D.
### Baron Ashbourne
(1837–1913) Page 30

The son of a well-to-do Irish father, Mr. Gibson was born seven-and-forty years ago, and, although a third son, inherited the largest share of a large fortune and a fair proportion of a good brogue. He distinguished himself both at school and at Trinity College, Dublin, as a plucky, self-asserting, industrious, and able youth, and, being called to the Irish Bar, he soon displayed all the qualities for success; for he was the son of an attorney, and he had prematurely white hair which gave him an air of maturity. He was very successful, and at five-and-thirty he became a Q.C. He had moreover given proof of possessing exceptional powers as a speaker, and in 1874 he essayed to enter Parliament for Waterford. Beaten there, he was put up for Dublin University in 1875, and after a hard struggle was elected to the seat which he has since held. His means enabled him to devote himself thenceforth to public life, and he soon showed that in him a new light had arisen among the Conservatives. He was at once made Attorney-General for Ireland, and, having for the last five years made some of the best speeches both in and out of Parliament on the Conservative side, he has now been appointed by the incoming Conservative Ministry as Lord Chancellor of Ireland.

Mr. Gibson is a sound lawyer, an earnest politician, and a persistent man. He has a fine voice, is a very good speaker, and has done an excellent service to the Conservative cause; yet he has somehow failed to establish himself as a distinct popular personality among the people at large. He is personally a most pleasant companion, he tells dry stories with dry humour, and he is always shrewd and astute in counsel. He is wise, and he looks it.

### Mr. Samuel Pope, Q.C.
(1826–1901) Page 31

An Irishman by race, brogue, and humour, Mr. Pope was born so long ago that the event has by common consent been forgotten. He was called to the English Bar in 1858, and made a Queen's Counsellor in 1869, and he brought qualities to his profession which have made him the leader of that department of legal practise before Parliamentary committees which is known to lawyers as "the Bear Garden." He is also the Recorder of Bolton, and one of those Benchers of the Middle Temple for whose abolition the rising junior barrister is now agitating. Moreover he is the Honorary Secretary of the United Kingdom Alliance. But he is not a teetotaller.

Mr. Pope has the ordinary culture and manners of the Bar; he is much experienced in Parliamentary practise, and greatly given to showing his experience by digging up old cases; he has a rich, vulgar, effective humour; and he is good-tempered and persuasive. His friends call him "Sam"; the Bar call him "Jumbo"; and he is altogether a good fellow of the Irish variety.

### Sir James Taylor Ingham, M.A., Knt.
(1805–1890) Page 32

The Chief Magistrate at Bow Street was born in the year in which the reign of King George the Third was glorified by the Battle of Trafalgar; consequently his early career is a matter of ancient history.

In the reign of King George the Fourth he was admitted as a student at the Inner Temple; and in the reign of King William the Fourth he graduated as an M.A. at Trinity College, Cambridge, and was called to the Bar. He joined the Northern Circuit and practised at the West Riding Sessions, most naturally, since his father—Mr. Joshua Ingham, late of Blake Hall and Knowle House— was a Yorkshire gentleman; but his prowess as an advocate has faded out of living memory.

Two years before Queen Victoria came to the Throne, he married a Miss Penrose, from Ireland; and in 1849 he was appointed one of the Magistrates of the Thames Police Court. In 1876 he succeeded

the late Sir Thomas Henry as the Chief of the twenty-three Metropolitan Police Magistrates, which position he still efficiently occupies, and was honoured with a Knighthood in return for his very protracted services.

He is a Justice of the Peace for the West Riding of Yorkshire, for Middlesex, and for Berkshire; he understands his business perfectly well, although his eighty-first birthday is over and gone; and there appears to be plenty of life in him yet.

Sir James Ingham is an ornament to the Magisterial Bench. His vast experience renders him extremely reliable in all that he does. He is an authority on International Law; wherefore cases involving points of difficulty under the various Extradition Treaties are always taken to Bow Street. His name is connected with all the Police Court *causes célèbres* which have arisen during the last dozen years, from the trials of the Dynamitists for treason-felony down to the investigation of the *locus standi* of the so-called proprietary gambling clubs. He displays a nose betokening much shrewd sense. His manner is courteous, with a quietly sarcastic tinge which is often very effective; yet he is a dignified Magistrate, never descending to that buffoonery which comes so ill from the Bench, and his Court is therefore always well ordered. He is a rival to Vice-Chancellor Bacon in his green and vigorous old age. He is a gentleman, and he draws a salary of £1800 a-year.

### The Rt. Hon. John Blair Balfour, P.C., M.P.
### Baron Kinross of Glasclune
(1837–1905) Page 33

Hard on fifty years ago a Clackmannan minister found himself the father of a son. The infant, on being christened, proved to be John Blair Balfour. Though diminutive of stature and shrill of voice, John Blair speedily developed some of the best characteristics of the middle-class Scot. He made good use of his education at the Academy at Edinburgh; he passed through the University of the same city, and, when twenty-four years old, he was called to the Scottish Bar. Being a well-behaved and canny young man, he contrived to marry the daughter of a Scotch Judge, and, being endowed with a hard head and a voluble tongue, he was much sought after, to the advantage of his banking account, by solicitors and writers to the Signet. When left a widower, his choice again fell upon a Judge's daughter, and three years later—in 1880—Mr. Balfour began to go up like the proverbial rocket. He became a Q.C.; he entered Parliament, and Mr. Gladstone conferred upon him the post of Solicitor-General for Scotland. The following year he was appointed Lord Advocate, and has held the office ever since, except during the few months while the Tories were in office. It is said by people who ought to be good judges that Mr. Balfour understands Scotch law. He is shrewd in debate, can explain obscure points in lucid language, and is urbane and courteous withal. He has never been known to lose his temper, but he occasionally offends by making a Caledonian joke. He is not an interesting man, but he has mastered the Crofters' Bill, he is a Doctor of Laws and a Privy Councillor, and he belongs to several Clubs. He will follow the example of his fathers-in-law and in the fulness of time become a Judge.

### Sir John Simon, Knt., M.P., Serjeant-at-Law
(1818–1897) Page 34

Descended from that ancient Oriental race, the members of which have shown so remarkable a gift of assimilating Western coin, habits, and ideas, Sir John Simon was born nearly seventy years ago in the Island of Jamaica. His immediate progenitors were planters, but it was early revealed to them that the infant Simon, instead of devoting himself to the cultivation of the sugar-cane, should proceed to England, there to grapple with the intricacies of our legal system. Accordingly, he found himself in due course eating dinners at the Temple; and his digestion being sound, he was called to the Bar without mishap. He moreover graduated at the London University (a rare achievement in those days), and, as he possessed certain influence among solicitors, he crept by degrees into a comfortable practise. At the mature age of fifty he fell an easy prey to political ambition, and entered the House of Commons as a

Member for Dewsbury—a borough which has displayed unaccountable fidelity by allowing him to represent it ever since. As true as Dewsbury has been to Sir John Simon, so true has Sir John Simon been to Mr. Gladstone, and he had just received his reward in the shape of a Knighthood, now only a few weeks old. Unlike many other Anglicised Jews, Sir John Simon continues to walk in the Hebrew faith, and his presence at the table of the House of Commons, with his hat on his head and the Old Testament in his hand, is a periodically recurring Parliamentary incident. He has no special claims to distinction, except that he is the only Member of the House who belongs to the almost extinct order of Serjeants-at-Law, and that a few years ago he was inaccurately reported to have departed this life. He is fond of good living, and given to hospitality. He is a prosy old gentleman.

### Sir Albert Kaye Rollit, Knt., LL.D., M.P.
(1842–1923) Page 35

The head of a prosperous firm of solicitors in London and Hull, Sir Albert Kaye Rollit owes something of his success to the circumstance that his father before him was likewise a solicitor of repute, but he owes still more to his own industry and long-headedness. Besides being a member of that lower branch of the legal profession identified from time immemorial with the sum of six-and-eight pence, he is a Doctor of Laws of two Universities, a Bachelor of Arts, an underwriter, a steamship owner, a Member of Parliament, a Fellow and Governor of King's College, a member of the Council of the Incorporated Law Society, and a Knight-Bachelor. Such leisure time as is at Sir Albert Rollit's disposal he utilises by amateur star-gazing as a Fellow of the Astronomic Society, by studying the habits of beasts of prey as a Fellow of the Zoological Society, and by investigating the ways of the finny monsters of the deep as Vice-President of the National Fish Culture Association at South Kensington. As a student he carried off one of the gold medals given by the London University, and since then his career has been an unbroken record of material and social advancement. Hull and Sir Albert Rollit—Sir Albert Rollit and Hull—are almost convertible expressions. He has been Town Clerk of Hull; he is an Alderman of Hull; he has been Sheriff of Hull; he has been twice Mayor of Hull; he could have worn the civic chain for a third time had he been so disposed—indeed there is little doubt that, if Hull were privileged to issue patents of nobility under the Corporate Seal, Sir Albert Rollit would be its first proud Duke. From all this it might be surmised that Sir Albert Rollit is a patriarch in years; but in truth he is a stripling, being yet only forty-four. South Islington sent him to the House of Commons last July, but the House of Commons continues to await his maiden speech. His Knighthood, of which he is very proud, came to him through his connection with the jubilee of municipal corporations. He is a widower, and a Conservative of the modern, progressive type. He knows a number of smart people, and is sometimes invited to stay at their places in the country, where he succeeds in making himself agreeable. He is active, pushing, and full of energies and side-lights, and hides none of them under a bushel.

### Mr. Justice William Ventris Field
### Baron Field of Bakeham
(1813–1907) Page 36

Sir William Ventris Field was born at Fielden, in Bedfordshire, four-and-seventy years ago, and is therefore amongst the most venerable of Her Majesty's Judges. He enjoyed a private but very useful education, being articled in his youth to a solicitor at Exeter, from whose office he presently migrated to London, to be there entered upon the roll of attorneys and solicitors. Three years of practise in this capacity fitted him for admission to the Honourable Society of the Inner Temple, by whom he was called to the Bar in 1850, when, like other wise barristers who have made to themselves friends of the Mammon of the Law, he got briefs. As he showed energy and capability in the conduct of the commercial cases, his practise grew; so that, in 1864, he was not refused "silk" when he asked for it. As a leader, Mr. Field developed into a remarkably good cross-examiner, which would hardly have been expected

from his antecedents; and many are the stories which are still told of his witty sallies and of his ways and means with hostile or otherwise refractory witnesses. He was always hard to get over; and when Lord Cairns (to the surprise of the profession, but to his own credit) made him a Judge in 1875, he soon showed himself to be as wide-awake as ever. Being a sound lawyer and an honest man, he abhors all shams, and pretenders never succeed in his Court. But it is as an authority in Practise and its mysteries that Mr. Justice Field has earned for himself great fame during life, if not after death. He knows and understands the intricate Rules of Court much better than most of his brethren do, and they—which is much more—know that he does so. Thus it is that he sits oftener than any other Judge at Chambers, where he displays much good sense but more bad temper. He is gifted with a particularly unmelodious voice, and he has a very strong aversion to being interrupted or "assisted" when reading an affidavit or otherwise engaged in a case. Consequently, if a very young Counsel, who happens to be ignorant of these little ways, should attempt in his innocence to explain to this Judge what he wants, he will infallibly be made to jump half out of his shoes by the very gratingly ejaculated but well-known wheeze, "Stay, please!" which everyone who has once heard it always associates with this Judge. Nevertheless his Lordship is not disliked, for his temper is known to be due to a painful infirmity, and he is in reality a good soul. Were he a younger man he would be promoted to the Court of Appeal, for which he is quite good enough. He is fond of horses and dogs, and he has been known to speak sarcastically to a less than usually intelligent jury. But he is a painstaking man on his "good" days, and he is not, like some of his brethren, altogether at sea in Chancery matters. He is a great pulveriser of frivolous defences; but he is a very deaf Judge, and often tries people in more ways than one.

### Mr. Charles Isaac Elton, Q.C., M.P.
(1839–1900) Page 37

The Eltons are a very respectable West Country family, and from a mother who was the daughter of a Baronet, and a father who was in the East India Company's Service, there was born eight-and-forty years ago Charles Isaac. Charles Isaac was instructed at Cheltenham and went to Balliol College, Oxford, where he worked hard and took a First Class in Law and Modern History, and a Second Class in Classics, besides gaining the "Vinerian" Law Scholarship. At six-and-twenty, having previously taken the precaution to marry, he was called to the Bar, and entered upon a career of hard, plodding work upon dry subjects, which was destined to make him an eminent authority on the law of Real Property. He has written dull but learned books on "The Tenures of Kent," and on the mysteries of Copyhold Tenure and the Court Roll, as well as on "The Origins of History," and has succeeded with the success which belongs to learned industry in a trivial and ignorant generation. In 1884 he was elected for a division of Somersetshire, a portion of which county he still represents. Being a man of weight and substance, who scales some thirty stone, a learned lawyer, and a statesman of intelligence, he is necessarily a Tory, and should properly be a Judge. He is a lively companion and popular.

### Mr. Frank Lockwood, Q.C., M.P.
(1846–1897) Page 38

Great-grandson of a respectable stonemason who afterwards became Mayor of Doncaster, he was rough-hewn in the same Yorkshire town about one-and-forty years ago, and his ends were shaped at the Manchester Grammar School and Caius College, Cambridge. Leaving the latter seat of learning with rather less knowledge than when he went up, he migrated to Lincoln's Inn, and in due course was added to the overstocked profession of the Bar, in which however, by reason of a ready wit, a bluff and wholesome presence, a rich voice, a good deal of law, and some self-confidence, he managed to make headway. Finding his talents wasted at the Chancery Bar, where on one occasion he nearly caused the late Lord Romilly to have a fit, he laid himself out for advocacy. He defended the malefactor affectionately known to juvenile students of criminal literature as

"Charley Peace"; he tickled North Country juries with his jokes; he cross-examined with shrewdness and effect; until at length without him no case of libel, breach of promise, or horse-coping was complete. After ten years as a Junior—during which period of probation he executed the best and most beneficial contract of his career by marrying a daughter of the house of Salis-Schwabe—he "took silk." Such an early venture would have been risky for a man less well provided for; but with Mr. Lockwood it was a complete success. And he is now one of the leaders of the Bar, and one of the best-liked men in England.

Turning his eyes Parliament-wards, he contrived to get defeated at Lynn; but now he sits for York as one of that self-denying flock of politicians whose Mecca is Mid-Lothian. He can make a capital electioneering speech; as an expert handler of witnesses he is unsurpassed; and he is the idol of the Junior Bar, for whose edification he covers reams of paper with pen-and-ink sketches. He never makes the mistake of sending a Judge a caricature of himself, but always that of a learned brother. He rides better than he shoots, and talks much better than he rides; but he is a sportsman to the backbone, and the burning of his grouse moor near Scarborough the other day is a misfortune which has gained for him the sympathy of all his friends. He labours under the suspicion of having once been a Tory, but he has taken more pains to deny the impeachment than its gravity perhaps warrants. He is a thoroughly good all-around man.

### The Rt. Hon. Henry Matthews, Q.C., M.P.
### Viscount Llandaff
(1826–1913) Page 39

Of Irish parentage, Cingalese birth, Parisian education, and Romish religion, Mr. Matthews entered upon life with valuable and various capacities and experiences. He was born one-and-sixty years ago, went to the Bar at four-and-twenty, and soon showed such ability and such "bite" of his cases as to achieve a reputation as an advocate and to be employed in various notorious law-suits. At two-and-forty he was still a Liberal, with a tendency towards the mild form of Irish Home Rule of that day; and, as such, was elected for Dungarvan in 1868. He retained this seat for six years, but, having subsequently contested it unsuccessfully at three elections, he renounced it and Ireland, reconsidered the situation by the light of the more dangerous and rebellious developments of the Home Rule Conspiracy, and became a Tory. Being retained in the Aston Park Affidavit case, he attracted the attention of Lord Randolph Churchill, who marked the clever lawyer for his own, and got for him, at Birmingham itself, in 1886, the first Tory seat that town had ever filled, and immediately afterwards the post of Secretary for the Home Department in Lord Salisbury's Government. This was a surprise to many, and a disappointment to some; but Mr. Matthews has done the work of his office fairly well, and has survived in the Cabinet the suicide of his original patron. He is, indeed, a man of considerable ability, yet in Parliament and before the public he has not been so successful as he should have been; for he is a lawyer-minded man, with more knowledge of courts and cases than of human nature, and with little of that sense of popular feeling which enables a politician to appear to lead those whom he follows. Hence the criticism and complaints, which never fail to fasten on a Home Secretary, have pursued him with especial vigour and some good grounds, in both the Cass case and the Lipski case; have bred the conviction that he is squeezable; and have encouraged future attempts to squeeze him. In private life he is the most amiable of men, and of improving and entertaining commerce. He has some quaint mannerisms of the unrehearsed kind. He is rich. He drives a mail-phaeton. He is a bachelor.

### The Hon. Sir Edward Ebenezer Kay
(1822–1897) Page 40

Born to Sir Robert Kay, Esq., of Rochdale, Lancashire, six-and-sixty years ago, Sir Edward Ebenezer Kay has since played successively the parts of Cambridge undergraduate, son-in-law of the late Master of Jesus, law reporter, Queen's Counsel, Chairman of the Quarter Sessions, Judge of the High Court, and, above all, protector of the widowed and fatherless.

He does not come of a public school, but he has missed no opportunity of assimilating equity and (since he has been a Judge) of cutting down legal costs in all directions. His unjudicial career lasted until 1881, when, after having practised as a "special" before the House of Lords for three years, he was raised to the Bench (which had just been vacated by Vice-Chancellor Malins) by Lord Selborne, who has since had no reason to regret the appointment.

Mr. Justice Kay is pre-eminently a Judge with a special mission. He is very fond of disallowing costs on the slightest provocation. It is always the duty of his Court "to protect this fund," when, in administration of trust cases, costs are asked "out of the Estate." He often threatens to "take vigorous measures" to protect such funds, and no one doubts his will or his power to do so. Sometimes he goes too far in this "full determination" of his; then the Court of Appeals sets him right, and the last costs of that case are worse than the first. Lawyers do not like Mr. Justice Kay, and they say nasty things about his not having discovered his mission until he left the Bar for the Bench; but infants and widows owe him a debt of gratitude, and some of them are grateful to him, which is the surest sign that he has done very much for them. Beyond this Mr. Justice Kay differs from the average Judge only in his personal appearance, in his knowledge of Equity, and in his manners. He is gifted with a strong sense of his own importance, and strives, with considerable success, to look as good a Judge as he is. He is more than sufficiently dignified to excite extreme respect for that majesty of the Law which he never misses the smallest chance of vindicating, in season and out of season. His knowledge of Equity is abstruse, and he seems to remember all the details of all the cases reported in "Kay's Reports" and "Kay and Johnson's Reports," by which he long ago immortalised the name of Kay. But his manners are imperfect. He has often been rude to counsel; he delights to say nasty things of and to solicitors; and he frightens witnesses. His voice grates, and his manner repels. He has a long upper lip which he is able to wreathe with an unpleasant curl. He is a martinet. He is a godsend to the Incorporated Law Society, which keeps a list of his more robust utterances ever ready to hurl at the heads of straying sheep of its rather mixed flock. But he is a good and strong Judge, who is able to get through a cause-list with equal celerity and certainty.

**The Hon. Sir Arthur Charles**

(1839–1921) Page 41

The seventh son of the late Robert Charles, Esq., he was born eight-and-forty years and a fortnight ago. He was sent by his father, who was a Londoner, to University School, and thence to University College, where he associated with various other embryo Queen's Counsel. Having become a London B.A., he chose the legal profession, and was called to the Bar by the Inner Temple in 1862, when he joined the Western Circuit. After several briefless years, his good genius moved him to law reporting. And from the staff of the *Weekly Reporter* he was soon promoted to that of the authorised Law Reports. He then picked up more law than briefs, and he might have continued briefless to the end had not a certain Judge once asked him to undertake the defence of a friendless murderer. Mr. Charles did not succeed in robbing the gallows of his client, but he did succeed in impressing the Judge favourably, and in consequence was presently made a Revising Barrister. After this he gradually emerged from obscurity, and when the present Lord Justice Lopes took silk, he came in for a good deal of junior work on Circuit, being retained in the great foreshore case by the Corporation of Exeter. Still following in Lord Justice Lopes' tracks, when the latter was elevated to the Bench, Mr. Charles took silk, and soon became the leader of his Circuit, earning especial fame as an Ecclesiastical lawyer. In 1878 he was made Recorder of Bath, and two years later he made an attempt to get into Parliament as a Member for his University; but being defeated by the present Lord Sherbrooke, he was successively made a Chief Commissioner to inquire into corrupt practices, a Royal Commissioner to inquire into the Ecclesiastical Courts, Chancellor of the Diocese of Southwell, Commissary to the Dean and Chapter of Westminster, and an honorary D.C.L. of Durham University; and finally, in September last, he was raised to the Bench, of which he is now the most youthful occupant, after having figured in all the prominent Ecclesiastical cases of his later years, from that of Martin v. Mackonochie to that of Mr. Bell-Cox, as well as in many cases of a more unholy nature, of which the *Mignonette* cannibal trial was the most sensational.

Mr. Justice Charles is still an untried Judge, but he has begun exceedingly well. He has the respect of the Bar, and he has dignity and ability. He has made a very successful *début* on the Old Bailey Bench, showing himself a just and impartial Judge, in the two important cases of unlawful assembly and of arson, which he just tried. At the Bar he was an eloquent advocate and a gentlemanlike opponent, and he is now in consequence a popular Judge. He has many friends; he is courageous; he is married; he is a sound Tory; and, like many other intelligent persons, he has a large nose.

**The Rt. Hon. Sir James Hannen, Knt., P.C. Baron Hannen**

(1821–1894) Page 42

Seven-and-sixty years ago, Mr. James Hannen, a worthy merchant in the City of London, was presented with his first-born son. He called him James, sent him to St. Paul's School—where he learned Latin with Mr. Baron Pollock—and later to Heidelberg University, where he learned other things. At the age of twenty-four, James became a student of the Middle Temple, then joined the Home Circuit, and, by a skillful combination of the family knowledge of commerce with his own of law, soon showed himself a reliable conductor of a commercial case. Having once shown this, his reputation grew, in spite of much and strong competition, until he attained devildom. He made a big mark as Counsel for the successful claimant in the great Shrewsbury case before the House of Lords, and he continued to make other big marks in many celebrated cases, until, having unsuccessfully opposed a Member of the Tory Government in a General Election, Mr. Disraeli made him a Judge of the Queen's Bench.

As a Judge, Sir James has figured in even a greater number of celebrated cases than he did as a Counsel. His typical judicial bearing marked him out as the successor to Lord Penzance, and in 1872 he stepped into that Judge's place in the Court of Probate and Divorce, whence he has since blossomed into the three-cornered President of the since-constituted Probate, Divorce, and Admiralty Division. As a Probate and Divorce Judge, he has always been all that can be desired; and even in Admiralty actions he has now managed to get well under way, and delivers judgements in collision cases of the hardest swearing with a lucidity which would do credit to any landsman. His knowledge of the world, his logical mind, his impartial nature, his capacity for correctly gauging the value of evidence, and his strong sense of justice, all combine to make him a perfect Daniel; and few Judges have been less criticised than Sir James has during the forty years of his dispensation.

But withal he is a domesticated man, fond of his own fireside, who eschews what is called Society. Possibly he sees enough of it in the Court over which he presides so strongly. For he is a solemn Judge, from whom none expects a joke or even a smile. He has many little ways of his own which have to be followed by those who practise before him. He is a contemplative Judge with a serene face. He has a strong objection to being called Mr. Justice Hannen, and he has a son at Cambridge who rowed in last month's University Boat Race.

**The Rt. Hon. Lord Justice Henry Cotton**

(1821–1892) Page 43

He was born sixty-seven years ago at Leytonstone, where lived the worthy merchant, William Cotton, who took the responsibility for the event. Being sufficiently provided with trade instincts by pedigree, his father sent him to Eton, where he passed the intervals between fagging for young Lords in judicious sapping. Going thence to Christ Church, he did better than most young men of his antecedents by taking a Mathematical First Class and a Classical Second, after which exploits he was called to the Bar, and so finally shook off from his feet the golden dust of commerce. At Lincoln's Inn his prospects were good, and he made the most of them. A very hard and conscientious worker, the dry forms of Equity drafting and conveyancing suited him, and he soon became known as a very skillful master of legal jargon. By the time he took silk, after twenty years of untiring drudgery, he was recognised in the profession as one of the safest practitioners on record, and quite the most honest. He became leader in good old Vice-Chancellor's Malin's Court; he migrated as a special fee man to the Privy Council; he became a Bencher at Lincoln's Inn; and he succeeded Lord Selborne as Standing Counsel to his University, which is a very honourable and distinguished position. Finally, when every possible honour had been conferred upon him, he conferred one on his country by becoming a Lord Justice over the heads of all the puisne Judges of the time.

Lord Justice Cotton has now been hearing appeals for ten years, and his judgements are all models of lucid reasoning, which ought to be bound up together in a large and handsome volume. He knows more of Chancery practise than any other living man, and is the best Real Property lawyer now on the Bench. His manner is academic and his politeness excessive; but he is as entirely free from the extreme suavity of the Lord Chief Justice as he is from the worldly knowledge of the Master of the Rolls. Very learned and rather simple, he is easily imposed upon as a man without guile; for his connections have always been so respectable that he refuses to believe in the existence of the unrespectable, until he is obliged to do so; and it is not easy to oblige him. His sole fault is his extreme simplicity; and as he has great and deserved influence over his fellow Lords Justices, who sincerely respect him, applications are sometimes granted on appeal which have been most properly refused by the Court below. He has a great horror of prevarication; he is very straight-laced; he is the soul of honour; and altogether a most respectable and most respected Judge. He is a quiet, unaggressive man, very sedate in company, and not given to the frivolities of Society, and has not, nor ever had, athletic tendencies, yet he is sometimes seen outside on a tame horse in the Row. He is the embodiment of honesty and law.

**The Hon. Sir John Charles Frederick Sigimund Day**

(1826–1908) Page 44

Born of a Dutch mother at the Hague two-and-sixty years ago, he commenced his education at Friburg, continued it at a Roman Catholic academy at Bath, went on with it at London University, where he took his B.A., and at the Middle Temple, which he joined at the age of nineteen, and is now completing it on the Bench. He was "called" in 1849, and he was soon chosen. He saw great opportunity in the attempt to clear away the then procedure muddle by the Common Law Procedure Act, which came to pass a few years after his call; and he seized it by writing a good book on the subject, which made him an authority on the old Rules of Procedure as long as they existed. He also indited a new edition of Roscoe's "Nisi Prius," and thus became a recognised authority on the Law of Evidence. So, having compassed an excellent practise on the South-Eastern Circuit, he gave up book-making and confined his attention to clients, who multiplied around him, as he gradually waxed greater, until eighteen years ago, when he was nominated a Queen's Counsel after three-and-twenty years of plodding and lucrative industry at the Bar. Ten years later he was asked to ascend the Bench; which he would have been asked to do long before had he been sufficiently a child of this world to be a politician.

He was a very skillful, a very vivacious, and a very witty advocate; but he is now less vivacious, and his wit has entirely evaporated, though he still often says things that are laughed at because it is supposed that they are intended to be laughed at. He never sought political honour, or dishonour, in the days of his advocacy; but politics have been put upon him in those of his judgement. A good deal of political mud has been thrown at him during the present year, of which, however, little, if any, seems to have stuck. In his criminal capacity he gives prisoners a fair trial and sees that they get it; but, when convicted, he shows them no mercy, and has been, on occasion, pretty freely abused in some quarters for administering very heavy sentences for very small crimes. He is a good Judge, and strong enough to be above sentiment; and none but the most unfledged of Counsel ever attempts the smallest piece of claptrap before him. He is also a good lawyer, and a good judge of human nature. Like his brother Mathew, he is a Roman Catholic by persuasion; in spite of which he has been very rudely and very unnecessarily, though very vainly, objected to as one of the Commissioners now sitting upon certain charges and allegations which have been made against certain Irish agitators, who thought, first, that the law of the land was not good enough for persons of their standing, and, secondly, that Mr. Justice Day was not a good enough Judge to discuss their exceeding merit; but he did signal service to the Government as First Commissioner on the Belfast Riots two years ago, and he may be depended upon now to do his duty in the new state to which it has pleased the Government and Providence to call him. He is an upright, sensible, and magnificently ugly man. He is above Society. He is very practical; and he has been on the treadmill.

### The Hon. Sir Archibald Levin Smith
(1836–1901) Page 45

He is the son of the late Francis Smith, Esq., J.P., of Salt Hill, Chichester, whose wife was a Miss Levin of the same place; and he perpetuates the names of both parents. Born in 1836, educated at Eton and Trinity, Cambridge, he was called to the Bar eight-and-twenty years ago, when he commenced the successful career which has lately culminated in his appointment as Third Commissioner to inquire into the journalistic Charges and Allegations the truth of which is now being so tediously investigated in Probate Court I. of the Royal Courts of Justice. His education failed to make either a prig or a great scholar of him; but his legal experience and sound common sense have since combined to make him a Judge who has no superior amongst his puisne brethren. His rise has been as rapid as deserved; for he showed enough practical sense in his conduct of such cases as fell into his hands early in his career to impress Lord Justice Bowen, then Attorney-General's "devil," with his quality, and, as a consequence, he became himself an imp of less degree, being appointed the devil's devil. That was all that was necessary to make the man, and when his master soared up to the Bench, Mr. Smith became a full-blown devil, in which capacity he counseled the Treasury so wisely that five years ago he was rewarded by being promoted to the position which he now occupies over the heads of all the Queen's Counsel of the day.

He is not a very brilliant man, but his mental grasp is most comprehensive. He drinks in a new Act of Parliament while other men skim its first section, and intricate accounts on a big commercial case are a delightful exercise to his well-trained mind. He is very lucid, very popular, very good-natured, and very free from serious fault. He never acts, never wastes time, and never sermonises even to criminals when they are found guilty before him. He does not respect persons, he does not advertise, nor does he shirk the most unpleasant work. All of which is high praise, but merited both by what he does and by what he does not. Not having the gift of tongue in any marked degree, his charges to juries are choppy and occasionally monotonous; but, being brief, clear, and always to the point, they are none the worse for that. There is only one more youthful Judge on the Bench; but there is also, take him for all in all, only one better. Being wealthy, he works rather for the good of others than himself; and having never been corrupted by Parliament, or by any other form of politics, he is extremely well adapted for the temporary office which he now occupies. He is always courteous even to the more foolish, and consequently more irritating, among juniors. He has much high spirit and much muscular strength; and his shoulders are types of the tremendous, with which he did stout service in the Cambridge Eight. He still loves exercise and the fresh air of Sussex. He is a jolly good fellow, who looks more like a sturdy English Squire than like the good Judge that he is. He is well favoured in all senses; and he wears a pair of *pince-nez* at the end of his nose.

### The Rt. Hon. Lord Edward Beckett (Denison) Grimthorpe, Q.C., LL.D.
### Baron Grimthorpe
(1816–1905) Page 46

Incredible though it may seem, Lord Grimthorpe was once upon a time an infant in arms. The year after the Battle of Waterloo his godfathers and godmothers named him Edmund, after his father, Sir Edmund Beckett Denison, a sturdy Yorkshire Baronet, who for many years represented the West Riding in the House of Commons. At Eton he began and at Cambridge he continued the course of studies which, in his seventy-fourth year, he does not regard as by any means finished. He gained a scholarship at Trinity, and became a Bachelor at the age of twenty, when he turned aside into the arid paths of the Law. Five years later he was called to the Bar at Lincoln's Inn, and proceeded to practise before Parliamentary Committees, where he speedily gained a reputation for thoroughness, shrewdness, and hard common sense. It was about that time that the railway mania took possession of English speculators, and Mr. Beckett Denison reaped, in the form of fees, his share of the money which then circulated so freely. In 1854 he became a Queen's Counsel, and, as older men dropped out, his native force of character, allied with a dash of truculence and a thorough mastery of detail, fashioned him into the acknowledged head of the Parliamentary Bar. Weak Committees he dominated by strength of will; strong Committees he cajoled; until at length the promoter or opponent of a Private Bill who had taken the precaution to retain Sir Edmund Beckett—for he dropped the "Denison" on succeeding to the Baronetcy—felt that his case was already half won. Seven or eight years ago he retired from practise, and he has since become a Peer.

Lord Grimthorpe is a many-sided man—a keen and somewhat bitter controversialist, a practical mechanic, a voluminous writer on diverse topics, a student of men and books, and Chancellor and Vicar-General of York. He is so high an authority on Church architecture that he is credibly reputed to know the difference between a gargoyle and a flying buttress. Under his direction the new works at St. Alban's Cathedral have been carried out; and the bells and "Big Ben" at Westminster owe their parentage to his versatile talent. His treatise on "Clocks, Watches, and Bells" has delighted the soul of the British Horological Institute, over which he presides; bell-founders regard him as an oracle; and his antagonists in the correspondence column of the *Times* tremble at his name in print. Yet he has leisure which he has occupied in teaching astronomy without the aid of mathematics. He is the designer of his own quaint raiment as well as of a number of churches; he is reputed to be very rich; he dispenses charity on scientific principles; and he has firm faith in the Church of England as by law established, and in Lord Grimthorpe. Mentally and physically he is a very tough old gentleman. He married a daughter of Dr. Lonsdale, some time Bishop of Lichfield; and he has written his father-in-law's life. He is not a Radical.

### Sir George Russell, M.P., D.L.
(1828–1898) Page 47

Towards the close of the seventeenth century there settled at Dover one Michael Russell, a sturdy Worcestershire Roundhead, who fought for Cromwell in the wars; and from him has come down a goodly host of Anglo-Indian administrators, Justices of the Peace, county gentlemen, and Barristers-at-Law, relieved now and then by a Victoria Cross hero and a County Court Judge. One of his descendants, Henry Russell, some time chief of the Supreme Court of Bengal, returned to England in 1812, whereupon he was forcibly converted into a Baronet. His son who was also named Henry, was for many years British Resident at the Court of Hyderabad; and he, in turn, had several sons, of whom this George was the third. As befitted one who, in those days, was without prospect of succeeding to a Baronetcy and its accompanying estates, the young man, after going through the educational mill at Eton and Exeter College, Oxford, was called to the Bar, and applied himself with so much industry to his clients and his briefs that, in due course of time, he found himself able to marry a niece of the late Duke of Richmond and to sit upon the County Court Bench of Circuit

No. 49; whence he dispensed cheap justice, until, through the death of his father and his brothers, he became the head of his house, when he withdrew from the adjudication of provincial squabbles over small debts, and was elected to serve in Parliament as one of the Members of the County of Berks. He continues to keep in touch with his old profession by acting as Recorder of Wokingham, the principal town in the Division which sends him to the House of Commons. In politics, he is a Conservative of moderate and enlightened views, and he is deservedly very popular in his county. He is one of those who hold that the work of legislation is not advanced by prolixity or frequency of speeches; his manners are courtly; he is without pomp or pride; and his years are about one-and-sixty.

### Mr. John Patrick Murphy, Q.C.
(1831–1907) Page 48

While the young John Patrick was yet a student of Trinity, Dublin, Patrick M. Murphy, Irish Queen's Counsel, very properly determined to send his eldest son to the English Bar, thereby faithfully foreshadowing those Unionist proclivities which are now causing a real Irish Murphy to support by his advocacy certain serious charges and allegations which have been made by a newspaper against a group of would-be Separatists. This Murphy was duly called by the Middle Temple in the year after the Crimean War, since which time he has been chosen by many to advocate their claims or to defend their rights; more especially by those who appreciate the influence which is exercised by his paternal ways upon the susceptible British jury, or who desire a sympathetic exposition of their wrongs. Twenty years of forensic climbing have brought him to the dignities of a silk gown and a seat amongst the Benchers of his Inn.

Mr. Murphy is not a great lawyer, nor is he a man of fashion; but he has several good qualities. He is jovial, popular, and chivalrous towards distressed damsels. If he has to advocate the claims of a lady who has been wronged, he does so with a sympathy which makes him her grateful friend for life. He has been known to privately interview such a client before she went into the box with a kindly delicacy which put an end to tears and robbed the coming cross-examination of half its terrors. He does not gesticulate after the style of the tub-thumper, the finger-shaker, the windmill, nor of any other emphasiser of his utterances; but he talks to the Court in a quiet, fatherly way, which is often very effective. He is far more refined than he looks, and his natural pose in Court is less artistic than is that of many an inferior gentleman; so that the faithful pencil, unaided by the pen, does not in his case give a true impression of the man. He has a son, lately called to the Bar, who is a very precise, though considerably enlarged, reproduction of himself. He has also a place at Lairg, though he lives at Norwood. A true Irishman, he is a member of the Reform, and therefore presumably a Liberal; but he is an utter foe to the Separatists, although he has been seen with a shamrock in his button-hole on St. Patrick's Day.

### Mr. Alexander Meyrick Broadley
(1847–1916) Page 49

Born at Bradpole, in Dorsetshire, two-and-forty years ago, he was sent forward in the way he should go by his father—who is also a dignitary of the Church; which way led him to Lincoln's Inn, whither he arrived in 1866. There he dined and vegetated like any coming Queen's Counsel during that space which is supposed to transfer an uncertain amount of law from musty folios into ambitious young heads; so that precisely twenty years ago he was called to the Bar. Then he took himself and his acquired knowledge to Africa, where he became an advocate in the Consular Court of Tunis, imparted the principles of English law to such Africans and others as sought his help, and made the acquaintance of General Boulanger, whose staunch friend he remains to this day. When the French Invasion came about, he budded forth as advocate of the oppressed Bey, and as special correspondent of the *Times*. Then, infected with literary craving, he wrote a book on Tunis, which marked him out as the Senior Counsel for Arabi Pasha, in which capacity having well acquitted himself—as he has shown in another book—his services were retained by ex-Khedive Ismail, for whom, in conjunction with Sir William Mariott, he succeeded in settling a dispute with, and securing a considerable fortune from, the Egyptian Government.

Six years ago he abandoned Law for Literature, came to London, and began to worry the Editors of the reviews. He is now supposed to be closely connected with the *World*, in which newspaper he has "celebrated" a number of more or less distinguished persons in their own homes; so that Mr. Edmund Yates has come to look upon him as one of his ablest and most loyal lieutenants.

He is a man of the World, and he loves the World. His dinners at Cairo Cottage—which is full of Egyptian reminiscence—are good, and his parties are amusing. He is generally on view at first nights and at other social performances. He is a kindly man, always ready to do his friend a service.

He is still a bachelor.

### The Hon. Sir William Grantham

(1835–1911) Page 50

The late Mr. George Grantham, of Barcombe Place, near Lewes, became his father four-and-fifty years ago; and when he had given him such education as was to be obtained at King's College, took time to consider which of the professions might be best suited for the son of a county gentleman, and eventually decided in favour of the Bar, to which this Judge was duly called at the mature age of twenty-eight years. Fourteen years later he became a Queen's Counsel; another year made him a bencher of the Inner Temple; and, having well served his Party as the representative, first of East Surrey and secondly of Croydon, from 1874 to 1886, he at last entered into his reward in the shape of a judgement seat in the Queen's Bench Division of the High Court of Justice. He has been a Deputy-Chairman of Magistrates, and he is still a Justice of the Peace, as well as a terror to wrong doers of that more atrocious kind to deal with whose sins is beyond the power of mere magistrates.

At the Bar Sir William was great in compensation cases. Less brilliant than he was careful, industrious, and polite, he made many friends, whom, for the most part, he has kept. He had interest on the South-Eastern Circuit, which gave him a start; and, as the years went on, his old-fashioned, pump-handle style of oratory became quite familiar in the Courts. He was not a great lawyer, but he made the best of things—including himself; and he has never been known to lose his temper. As a Judge, he has not been an unmitigated success; for he is sometimes overruled by the court above him, and he has occasionally expressed himself too plainly for some people; as when he set the Principality by the ears, by asserting that the Welsh were liars. He holds strong views as to the proper treatment of criminals, and makes an excellent Judge of criminal cases; and though his enemies said when he was elevated to the Bench that he was little qualified to be a Judge, no man among them was able to show that he had any particular disqualification for that office.

He is a genial sportsman, fond of shooting—which he does well—and of games; so that he has twice damaged himself while playing cricket. He knows something of agriculture, and has done much for his tenants, by whom he is beloved. He comes of an ancient family, and owns to an ancestor—one, St. Hugh Grantham—whom the Jews crucified at Lincoln in the good old days when Richard of the Lion Heart was King.

### Mr. James Vaughan

(1814–1906) Page 51

Bow Street has always been famous for the excellence of its police law; and never more so than when Ingham, Knight, and Vaughan and Flowers, Esquires, were its three Magistrates. And of these three but this one is now left.

He is the son of one Richard Vaughan, of Cardiff; and though his origin is lost in the dimness of early history, it is recorded that he was keeping terms at Oxford very nearly sixty years ago. There he was made a Bachelor of Arts; but presently he developed into a son-in-law of Jacob Bright, of Rochdale. He got himself called to the Bar at the Middle Temple; and, having served as Chairman of two Election Commissions under the old regime, he received his reward precisely a quarter of a century later. He has

now sat at Bow Street for six-and-twenty solemn years; outliving most of those whom unkind circumstances have compelled to face him there. He is Deputy-Lieutenant for Chorley, and Justice of the Peace for five counties; and he has been twice married.

He is a very kindly man, as well as an excellent Magistrate; and it is only the most hardened offender who is unable to entertain some respect for him. The casual tippler knows him, and appreciates the grave kindness of the old catch phrase, "Don't come here again," so highly that he very often does go there again.

### Sir Hardinge Stanley Giffard
### Earl of Halsbury

(1823–1921) Page 52

The third son of Stanley Lees Giffard, he is one of an old Devonshire family, and one of the most fortunate of men. He began—sixty-five years ago—as Hardinge Stanley Giffard, took a bad degree at Oxford, and went to the Bar and the Old Bailey; he proceeded as Sir Hardinge Giffard and Solicitor-General—fifteen years ago; and he has ended by climbing on to the unexpected Woolsack a second time as a Tory Lord Chancellor and as nominal President of the Supreme Court of Judicature. And people have not yet ceased wondering how he did it at all.

The Criminal Bar is not remarkable as a nursery of great lawyers; and the only two Old Bailey Counsel who are known to have attained greatness unconnected with crime are Mr. Justice Hawkins and Lord Halsbury. But Mr. Giffard, being full of shrewdness, married an attorney's daughter, and resolved to make no enemies until he had grown great. He believes that faith may remove mountains; and his faith in himself is as limitless as his boldness is unabashed. He made money, and laid it out generously, for his Party and for himself; knowing that what he expended on four Parliamentary defeats in the old corrupt days was well spent money. And so the four times rejected Old Bailey counsel has become the head of the profession.

He was a clever handler of witnesses, and he knew how to manage a jury; but he is not a great lawyer. He began his civil practise and gained his reputation in the great Tichborne case, which made the fortunes of all the Counsel who were engaged in it. He has since appeared in many celebrated trials, and his strong point has always lain in the skillful management of his cases.

As a successor to Lord Hatherley, Lord Cairns, and Lord Selborne, he is not an impressive Keeper of the Queen's Conscience. He is without dignity, and he is distinguished neither for his good looks nor for his noble bearing. Yet, with all his imperfections, he is well pleased with himself; and he remembers his old friends to such purpose that he has been very rudely called "The Lord High Jobber."

### Sir John Bridge

(1824–1900) Page 53

He was born to Mr. John Bridge, of Dover, seven-and-sixty years ago; and having received a decent education he was sent to Trinity College, Oxford, of which University he is a graduate; and to the Inner Temple, whose Benchers called him to the Bar at the mature age of twenty-six. So, being started in life, he worked hard enough to attain a small Common Law practise, and behaved well enough to become a very popular member of the old Home Circuit. As wine steward to the Circuit mess he first showed that tact for which he has since been distinguished; giving satisfaction which is quite unusual among barristers, who are all judges of wine, yet always differ in their judgement.

Twenty years ago he was known as a sensible, good-natured man of the world, without knowledge of criminal law, in which he had never dabbled; and being thus qualified, he was put on the Magisterial Bench. He has since almost daily proved that the Old Bailey Counsel is not the best material from which to manufacture police magistrates. He is now the Chief Metropolitan Magistrate, a Bencher of his Inn, and a Knight; and he is generally regarded as an altogether excellent dispenser of petty justice.

He is a good fellow and a gentleman; which is not always the case with magistrates. He is also an ami-

able man, thought he is quite strong enough to keep his Court in order. He has a persuasive manner that is sometimes quite fatherly.

His pet abomination is the swindling philanthropist.

### Mr. Thomas Beard

(1828–1895) Page 54

He was born three-and-sixty years ago, and while still quite young he came to London to learn, in a solicitor's office, the significance of pink tape and the intricacies of the criminal law, until such time as he might practise on his own account. Since then he has defended, or has prepared the defence of, many wicked men: some of them so wicked that he could not save them; as were Franz Muller, who was hanged for the murder of Mr. Briggs in a railway carriage, and the mutineers of the *Lennie*. For more than twenty years he has been attached to the Corporation of London, being well known as a Chairman of Committees; and he is now serving as Under-Sheriff for the sixth time.

He is fond of the Play, and he is quite a popular man in the City, being looked upon as a good fellow. He has so much respect for the Law that he has put two sons into it; so that he now has most of his professional work done for him.

### Sir Peter Henry Edlin, Q.C., J.P., D.L.

(1819–1903) Page 55

Sir Peter, who was born at Mortlake two-and-seventy years ago, led the quiet life that befits the son of a county gentleman for eight-and-twenty years; then, there being no examinations in those days, he joined the Bar as a Middle Templar, went to India for a couple of years, returned to England, joined the Western Circuit, and was appointed a Revising Barrister. At the age of fifty he took silk, and a wife; became a Bencher of his Inn, and settled down to his profession. Not being friendless, he was presently made the Recorder of Bridgwater that he now is; and having been Assistant-Judge of the Middlesex Sessions for fifteen years he was Knighted, and converted into the Chairman of the new County of London Sessions. He is also a Justice of the Peace and Deputy-Lieutenant for Middlesex.

He is a Judge of so much character that not only do prisoners and Counsel disagree in their views as to his deserts, but even those who practise before him think differently of him. Half of his Court says that he is a very bad Judge indeed; the other and better half that he is a very good Judge indeed. Yet on one point all who know him are agreed; for none denies the severity of the sentences that he inflicts on guilty persons who have the bad luck to be brought before him. Yet his severity is more in the nature of merit than of fault; for it is his to deal with the more petty offences of the habitual criminal classes of the wickedest town in the world. He is a pompous, rather irritable Judge, who takes nobody's opinion but Sir Peter Edlin's; and therefore he may be regarded as a "strong" Judge, who will not allow himself to be bamboozled into error, nor badgered in the dispensation of Justice. He is rather inclined to be a bully in his own Court; but insomuch as the Bar of Middlesex Sessions—(which is now by promotion known as the Bar of the London County Sessions)—does not represent the flower of forensic chivalry, this is quite a wholesome thing. For it is better to bully than to be bullied, especially in the case of a Judge; and this Judge will neither brook the interference of paid advocates nor of Radical journalists: even when he is in a good temper.

He is a good Judge with some faults. Hardworking, honest, independent, he rightly makes the habitual criminal feel that the hand of Justice is a heavy hand; but he is undiscriminating enough and irritable enough to fall upon occasion into undesired error. Yet he is a Judge after the honest Englishman's heart. His voice is not agreeable; and his wig has seen service.

### Mr. Charles Willie Mathews

(1850–1920) Page 56

Born in New York two-and-forty years ago, he found his way, while still a boy to Eton; and in spite of the lack of that manner and voice which are said to be more valuable at the Bar than legal wisdom, he determined to tempt Fate and juries. He was called twenty years ago, and, being quite open to histrionic influence as the step-son of Charles Mathews the Younger Celebrated Comedian, he naturally chose that branch of the profession in which the ability to assume (on behalf of a client) a virtue if he had it not is a possession of worth. His father's popularity with the play-going Bar of the last generation got him devilment under Mr. Montagu Williams, who was himself by way of being a theatrical person; and having thus gotten a start, he went on and made a criminal practise at the Old Bailey and on the Western Circuit; improving himself so much that, when Mr. Poland was called inside the Bar, he became Junior Prosecuting Counsel to the Treasury.

In Court he has a mincing manner that is full of affectation; yet out of Court he is an unaffected little fellow. He has also an unpleasantly high-pitched voice; but for this his pleasantly keen face makes amends, while his cool urbanity has been a marked success. He is not in great repute as a pleader, but he can marshall evidence; and, when they have grown used to his voice and manner, he can compel juries. He has been retained in some big cases.

He is full of youth; yet it is common report that he may be expected to look thirty by the end of the century.

### The Rt. Hon. Sir Charles Synge Christopher Bowen, P.C., D.C.L., LL.D., F.R.S.
### Baron Bowen
(1835–1894) Page 57

Born to a Freshwater parson in the Isle of Wight seven-and-fifty years ago, he developed in quite early childhood remarkable talent, physical and mental. He was sent to Rugby, where he won races, played in the Eleven, joined the almost invincible football team, became Captain of the School, and, by way of incidental variation, took the Balliol Scholarship. This last exploit led him to Oxford, where he ran a course whose brilliance is yet uneclipsed. He won the Hertford, the Ireland, and the Latin Verse; he wrote the Arnold Prize Essay, and took First Classes in all his Schools; and, while waiting for his degree, he cantered off with a Balliol Fellowship. He went from Oxford to the Bar; joined the Western Circuit; and having "devilled" for a space for the present Lord Chief Justice—(thereby improving his master's reputation)—he became Junior Counsel for the Treasury and was a made man. He was the Senior Truck Commissioner in 1870; fashioned into Recorder of Penzance in 1871; and improved into the most youthful Judge on record before he had taken silk, at forty-four. He has been honoured with a Commemoration degree at Oxford, and he is Visitor of his old College.

As a puisne Judge he was a failure with juries, who could not appreciate his cooing mildness any more than they could his distinctive niceties; but the British juryman is the only thing that he has ever been known to fail with. He has now for ten years been a Lord Justice, unequalled alike for his knowledge of Law and Equity; without rival in his ready grasp of hard cases or his quick solution of intricate problems; all but infallible; and a contriver of judgements that are models for their law, their English, their lucidity, and their strength. He is an unruffled Judge; too modest to be ever contemptuous, yet full of the most polite and gentle sarcasm. He has a masculine intellect, a sweet, low voice, a stupendous memory, a gentle, deprecating manner, and a round, large-eyed face which would do credit to a Bishop.

He is one of the few Judges who are known in Society; of which he is fond without frivolity. He is a cultured man of vast information, who can talk well on all worthy subjects; but he is so unassertive that he has been called shy. He is altogether the best lawyer in England; and when it loses him the Bench will lose its brightest ornament. He belongs to the Athenæum and University Clubs; and he has found time to make a scholarly translation of Virgil's Eclogues and of the First Book of the Æneid.

He has been very ill; but he is now happily progressing towards recovery.

### The Hon. Sir John Gorell Barnes
### Baron Gorell
(1848–1914) Page 58

He is the eldest son of the late Henry Barnes, shipowner, of Liverpool; he was born five-and-forty years ago; and, having taken a degree at Peterhouse, Cambridge, he began life in business. But it so irked him that at nine-and-twenty he got himself called to the Bar. He was called within it a dozen years later; and he was put upon the Bench of the Probate, Divorce, and Admiralty Division last year after only sixteen years of practise.

He is a solid lawyer who owes quick success to the happy accident (or design) by which he became attached to the chambers of the practitioner who is now known as Mr. Justice Mathew. For as an utter barrister that Judge (who never was a Queen's Counsel) revelled in the leading junior commercial practise; and Barnes, with his business experience, naturally found in him an instructor in legal practise. The two were alike in that they were both robust in body and robust in intellect, and Mr. Barnes owes his success to Mr. Gladstone; for when that elderly politician made a Judge of Mr. Mathew, Mr. Mathew's clients went to Mr. Barnes in a body; who encouraged them by looking forty-five, in spite of his three-and-thirty years, while in voice, manner, and figure he resembled his elevated master whose mantle thus fell upon him. By his Liverpool experience also he became so recognised an authority in shipping cases that when he took silk he also took a seat within the Bar of the Admiralty Court, and began to skim the cream of the Admiralty practise; being strong enough to brush aside even such rivals as Sir Charles Hall, Sir Walter Phillimore, and "Tommy" Bucknill. Yet he is commonly reported also to owe something to the Tories; for, though he did not dabble in Politics, he got a pupil in a son of Lord Salisbury's, and thereby obtained Conservative prestige. He was never very eloquent, nor is he a brilliant man; but he is learned, sound, and grave. Yet his gravity in Court has never been sepulchral (as was that of Mr. Gainsford Bruce) but rather jovial. When the layman who knows him finds it hard to discern wherein lay his legal merit, a lawyer will expressively tell him that "he carried weight": which is a pregnant phrase and a true.

He is a good Judge who gets through a great deal of work in a business-like way to the satisfaction of all who are concerned. He wears very solid spectacles which add very considerably to his dignity.

### Sir Henry Thring
### Baron Thring
(1818–1907) Page 59

He is the second of five sons born to the late Reverend John Gale Dalton Thring, of Alford House, in Somerset; of whom three became parsons, one, Edward, now dead, was the excellent and popular Head Master of Uppingham School, and, himself, Henry, after being grounded at Shrewsbury School, went to Magdalen College, Cambridge, and got third place in the Classical Tripos, became fourteenth Junior Optime and a Fellow of his College. Having achieved so much and being still most industriously inclined, he went to the Bar with qualities and luck that together some three-and-thirty years ago improved him into Counsel to the Home Office. Eight years later he rose to be Parliamentary Counsel; after which, as a matter of course, he was honoured with a K.C.B., and, when he retired from Office seven years back, he was very naturally offered a Peerage, which he accepted as the slight reward to which his years of service had entitled him from a grateful country.

He has now lived through precisely three-quarters of a century; but he found himself in the House of Lords too late to cut the figure that he might there have cut as a younger man. For he had been warped into detailed narrowness by a long life of drudgery, spent in the unwholesome drafting of Parliamentary documents, such as would have made musty the talents of a better man. Yet has he written much outside the routine work of his Office. Among many other Bills, he drafted the Joint Stock Companies' Acts of 1856, 1857, and 1858, the Joint Stock Banking Companies' Act of 1857, and the consolidation of those Acts by the Companies' Act of 1862; whereby he became, as he thought, qualified to contrive that work on "The Law and Practise of Joint Stock and Other Companies," which still, though much edited, bears his name; in which he explained to those concerned how the principle of Limited Liability was meant to work. He has also written on the Succession Duty Act, and on "Practical Legislation"; of the cler-ical part of which at least he should know as much as any man.

He lives at Egham, and he is a County Councillor for Surrey. He greatly interests himself in good works, and, being a keen politician as well as an ardent admirer of Mr. Gladstone, he conscientiously misses no chance of attending a Liberal meeting. He married a niece of Lord Cardwell, and having one daughter he has no heir. He is a very worthy man; but he does not go into Society.

### Mr. Arthur John Edward Newton
(1860–1907) Page 60

Born three-and-thirty years ago to the actuary and manager of the Legal and General Life Association, it may be presumed that he was distantly connected with things legal from his childhood; yet he did not at once take kindly to the Law. Educated at Hawtrey's and at Cheltenham—where he first earned schoolboy fame as a footballer—he was presently articled to Messrs. Frere, Forster, and Company of Lincoln's Inn Fields; but he learned more than clerical work before he was admitted. He travelled in London and visited New Zealand; and so learned something of the world. He qualified for practise nine years ago; but he has scarce practised for nine years, for he was not poor enough. Yet in the last seven or eight years he has made himself, by ability, industry, and decent manners, till he has come to employ a considerable staff in Great Marlborough Street, and to be employed by most of the persons of any note who may succeed, either by mischief or by ill-luck, in getting an introduction to that other Mr. Newton who, with Mr. Hannay, presides over the Great Marlborough Street Police Court. There he has successfully prosecuted bogus money-lenders and other defects of civilisation. There he has lately been involved in the cases of Dr. Collins and of Dr. Scott Saunders; and there he appeared in the prosecution that resulted from an attempt to swindle Lord Dudley. There, too, he has defended a multitude of foolish young men who, in a more or less disorderly way, have made the acquaintance of the police; and there he once got himself into trouble by too zealous defence of an undeserving client. He was not a man of great influence, and therefore his success is mainly due to himself; yet has he the great advantage of a good appearance which contrasts strangely with that of the ordinary type of Police Court advocate. He is not eloquent, but he is lucid; and though he is strong yet is he courteous. He misses few points; and it is the common opinion that he has deserved his success.

He claims descent from that Sir Isaac Newton who was supposed to have been the only man since Adam to connect an apple with the fall—until the modern iconoclast shattered the old story concerning the discovery of gravitation. With the exception of the Knight of Ely Place and of perhaps one other, he is the most widely known criminal solicitor in London.

He can swim; and he has more than once been found guilty of giving a conjuring entertainment.

### The Hon. Sir Lewis William Cave
(1832–1897) Page 61

He is a robust, satisfactory Judge, who gets through his work fast, makes up his mind quickly, and never alters his opinion; thereby constantly sending suitors (often with success) to the Court of Appeal. He frequently describes their argument as stuff and nonsense, yet Counsel like him; for so soon as he has made up his mind he is impartially brusque to both big and little. When a point is taken before him he is at once either with it or against it. In the former case he turns to the other side with a "What do you say to that?" In the latter event he says, "That won't do, you know. Have you nothing else?" And generally no answer to the wheeze is expected.

His father owned a small estate in Northamptonshire, upon which he was born in the year of the great Reform Act. He presently became a schoolfellow of Mr. Goschen at Rugby, and thereafter he left Oxford a Second-class Classics, and married a country parson's daughter on his way to the Bar. As a Counsel he soon earned a reputation for Chamber work; for he could state a case quickly, lucidly, and emphatically; and there being in those days less of dainty polish in the language of the Judge and Counsel, Mr. Cave's honest and good-natured rudeness did him no harm. But he did more than snap up unconsidered Orders. He worked hard, devoted his legal leisure to writing and editing law treatises, and gradually got together a sound practise of dimensions. Further, though he never did anything brilliant, yet he did nothing very foolish; so that no one was surprised when Lord Selborne put him on the Bench twelve years ago. Nor would anyone have been surprised had Lord Selborne not done so. Then Mr. Chamberlain by upsetting the old Bankruptcy Law, and Vice-Chancellor Bacon by declining to become a student of new law in his old age, gave him the chance of showing greatness as a Judge in Bankruptcy; which he has carefully avoided doing, by proving himself a tolerably satisfactory all-round Judge. For he carried all his virtues with him on to the Bench, and remains a good-natured, blunt person, so well satisfied with himself, his doings, and his position that he neither cares to amend his ways nor to grow great—except physically. He is at his best as a criminal Judge, before whom every man has a fair trial. He handles juries carefully and sensibly; he makes no fuss, and he never plays to the gallery. He is a good-humoured, sensible fellow, in whom are good points and no false sentiment; yet has he a deaf ear which is extremely useful when he has made up his mind.

He is a big, obstinate, strong, popular Judge.

**The Hon. Sir William Rann Kennedy**
(1846–1915) Page 62

He is a young Judge of seven-and-forty years, who became the eldest son of a country parson under a lucky star. Full of unjudicial weakness, despite his education at Eton, and at King's College (of which he was a Fellow), and at Pembroke, Cambridge (whence he graduated Senior Classic just thirty years ago), he has got on well; yet he does not greatly adorn the Bench. It was not until eight years after he left Cambridge that he got himself called to the Bar; but he did other work in the meantime, being for a year or so Private Secretary to the President of the Poor Law Board, and other things. When he did get called he went the Northern Circuit, and presently married a daughter of the Royal Academician, George Richmond. As a junior, he took pains in his profession, worked hard, and showed an earnestness that commended him as a careful trustee of his clients' interests. When he took silk eight years ago, he took little else, except at Liverpool, where he had a considerable practise in commercial and shipping cases. He has more ability than that which he has been generally credited; for as a Queen's Counsel of three years' standing he was offered an Indian Judgeship, but, thinking better of himself than other men thought of him, he declined the offer with thanks, on the very real ground, no doubt, that he was born to better things. And his sense was justified last year when a grateful Gladstonian Government made him a Judge of the Queen's Bench Division; partly (as his enemies say) because he was on excellent terms with the Lord Chancellor, more because other leading lawyers who deserved to be preferred before him had done nothing for their Party, or else had seats in the House of Commons which their Wise Old Leader feared to risk; and mostly because he had pluckily fought more than one Gladstonian fight, and luckily (for himself) had always suffered defeat.

He has now sat upon the Bench long enough to show that, with all his virtues, he is a failure as a Judge. He began by getting into a muddle over a felony in the country for that a juryman walked out of the jury-box during the trial; he has gone on fussily; and he is now approved the least "strong" of those who administer justice in the High Court. He is very hard-working, very honest, and very courteous to the Bar, so that he is liked in the Court more than he is respected; for the first thing needful in a Judge is to be able to judge. He would be at least an average Judge did he not suffer from so grave an inability to make up his mind that he often finds it very hard to come to any decision at all; yet is he so well liked for himself that fewer hard things are said of him as a Judge than are thought.

He is a very weak Judge with excellent intentions.

**The Hon. Sir Arthur Kekewich**
(1832–1907) Page 63

The late Samuel Trehawke Kekewich, of Peamore, Exeter, was Member of Parliament for the City of Exeter, and afterwards for South Devon; and two-and-sixty years ago he became the father of that second son, Arthur, who now helps to grace the Bench of Her Majesty's Judges. He was an Eton boy and a Balliol man; who when he had taken a First Class in Classics and a Second in Mathematics, was most appropriately made a Fellow of Exeter. Soon afterwards he was called to the Bar; and in the same year he married a daughter of the great solicitorial firm of Freshfields (who are solicitors to the Bank of England); and having successfully come to "silk" and become a Bencher of his Inn, and having very unsuccessfully contested two elections, Lord Halsbury (who himself is a Devonshire man) made him a Judge of the Chancery Division. He has now sat upon the Bench for some nine years, earning the respect of all who appear before him, if not a reputation for greatness.

Perhaps the wisest thing that Mr. Justice Kekewich ever did was to marry; for he married early and well. He began his career as junior Counsel for the Bank of England; and being a man of capacity he did all that was required of him, so that when he was called within the Bar he began to appear as leading Counsel for the Bank. There are few better clients than the Bank; yet he never had a very big practise, nor was ever very famous as a Counsel: not even famous enough to persuade the electors of Coventry, or of Barnstaple. But for all that he has done Lord Halsbury no discredit on the Bench. He is able to judge; for he can generally make up his mind to his own satisfaction, if less often to the satisfaction of others. He is also business-like, and for an equity lawyer (who generally thinks and acts with monumental slowness) he is quite rapid in his work. It was once said of him by a very learned and rather caustic ornament of the Court of Appeal, who, unhappily, is since dead: "He is an admirable Judge of first instance. He finds out at once what is the point of dispute, confines the case to that point, keeps out irrelevant matter, and decides the point quickly—and sometimes rightly."

He is a rather hasty Judge, whose manners are not always very pleasant. He is also a very good sort of fellow and so keen a golfer that he sold his billiard-table in order to utilise the room for the practise of driver and brassey with a captive ball.

**Sir Edward Macnaghten, P.C.**
**Baron Macnaghten**
(1830–1913) Page 64

He is one of those happy men who have never had to work hard; and his face shows it. At Cambridge he rowed in the eight; and as a silk he practised before Mr. Justice Chitty, who had rowed in the Oxford Eight. He has always been well off, and he became the husband of a Judge's daughter. Nevertheless he is a sound lawyer who has been heard to attribute his success at the Bar to the glassy eye of an old frequenter of the Court, which fixed itself upon him when he first rose, and put him on his mettle. Though he had a perfectly safe seat, it seemed ridiculous that he should be created a Law Lord when he had never been on the Bench, upon which was sitting such as a man as the late Lord Bowen, who ought to have gone up before him; nevertheless his elevation was no job, but quite an unexceptional appointment; and he has not discredited his high Office.

He is a good, cheerful fellow, an excellent host, and a kindly-hearted man.

**Mr. Anthony Hope Hawkins**
(1863–1933) Page 65

Younger son of the Rev. E.C. Hawkins, of St. Brides, and nephew of Mr. Justice Hawkins, he is now nearly two-and-thirty; and in his short life he has achieved a position among the best of our younger novelists that entitles him to a place in this gallery. He went up from Marlborough College to Balliol as a scholar, and when he had taken a degree, went to the Bar in order to learn to write. He wrote short stories for the papers; and five years ago he called his first book "A Man of Mark." Then he thought it good enough to write more books; and having written four of varying merit, he suddenly burst upon the world as something like a master of romantic fiction. But the success of "The Prisoner of Zenda" has done him no harm; for he now commands a good price, yet will not write more than he should, but is grown careful of his reputation. He once stood for Parliament and was beaten; yet he can make a good speech after dinner. He is a slim, quiet young man of domestic virtues, with a deep voice, and the look of an ascetic; who is not yet spoiled.

He calls himself "Anthony Hope"; and he is endowed with much versatility—on paper.

**Mr. Justice James Charles Mathew**
(1830–1908) Page 66

James Charles Mathew, Irishman and eldest son of the late Charles Mathew, of Lehena House, County Cork, and (though he was not himself a teetotaller) a near relative of the famous Father Mathew, was born five-and-sixty years ago. He is a T.C.D. man, who took High Honours; and was presently called to the Bar by the Honourable Society of Lincoln's Inn. Since then he has become a Judge, a husband and the Home Rule father of Mrs. Dillon. He has also been Chairman of the Irish Evicted Tenants' Commission and a Member of the Council of Legal Education and Chairman of the Board of Studies of the Inns of Court.

He is a good Judge, especially in commercial cases. As a junior barrister he became famous as a commercial man—so famous that he jumped over the Inner Bar to the Bench; being one of Mr. Gladstone's good choices. He is extraordinarily quick in seeing points, and so soon as he sees a point his mind settles it for him; so that he is little influenced by the arguments of Counsel—which is perhaps (in this case) no bad thing. It has been said indeed that he decides hastily; but, as he nearly always decides rightly, he is not greatly to be blamed for this. Nevertheless, when he is wrong, he is very wrong indeed; and this generally happens on points of Equity. For, being a business man as well as a lawyer, his abhorrence of Equity is only equalled by his ignorance of its principles; and hence it is that when the Judges sit in Council he is a terror to his brother Chitty, who, though he is another good lawyer, believes in the Chancery Division and long arguments. To Mr. Justice Mathew is due the credit of that new Commercial Court which is the single conspicuous success among modern attempts to revive public confidence in the Law Courts. He is pleased with this, but fails to perceive that it is not the Commercial Court, nor the Commercial Rules, that please suitors; but the Commercial Judge whom they like, receiving his decisions everywhere with respect.

He is a Judge who, knowing how to make up his mind, hate delays and quibbles. He is an imperious, obstinate, kindly Irishman, and a good after-dinner speaker.

**The Hon. Sir Alfred Wills**
(1828–1912) Page 67

A solicitor became his father eight-and-sixty years ago; wherefore he naturally went to the Bar. He also inherited brains; wherefore they made him a Fellow of University College (London). He became a barrister and a Bachelor of Laws in the same year; was called within the Bar at the age of forty-six, was made Recorder of Sheffield eight years later; and was improved into a Judge of the Queen's Bench a dozen years ago. Since then he has been President of the Railway and Canal Commission, Editor of "Wills on Circumstantial Evidence," Treasurer of the Honourable Society of the Middle Temple, and author of "Wanderings Among the High Alps" and of "The Eagle's Nest." For he is as industrious a Judge as he is a benevolent man.

He is so industrious indeed that he is said to have tried a treadmill; and so benevolent that he has tried (with some success) to improve our prison arrangements. He is a conscientious man and a conscientious Judge; so that he tempers Law with an amount of morality that has earned for him the degree of "Benevolence on the Bench." At the Bar he was so highly regarded by the more worldly solicitor that he was made Standing Counsel to the Incorporated Law Society; and when he left the Bar for the Bench none but his enemies (who are very few) had a word to say against his elevation. Yet is he no great lawyer, for he suffers from a constitutional inability to distinguish between the merely legal and the merely honourable; the result being that he is apt to apply the principles of Honour to affairs of Commerce: which, of course, is ridiculous. Thus, though he may benefit the community at large, he perplexes lawyers and horrifies men of the City. In a word, he administers Morality, whereas baser men say that he ought to administer Law. Nevertheless he makes much amend for his morality by his devotion to work; which passes the devotion of other Judges. With prisoners he is humane rather than merciful; for he is even more anxious that every prisoner should have his chance than he is to give every criminal his due. With the Bar he is very popular; for he is courteous to all, great and small alike. In the Long Vacation he climbs Alps with much credit; and he is so fond of fresh air and exercise that, while he keeps a serene forehead, his cheeks ever wear the apple-bloom of wholesome youth.

He is not a great Judge; but he is a good one. He looks the man that he is.

**Mr. Frederic Andrew Inderwick, Q.C.**
(1836–1904) Page 68
He was born to a naval officer sixty years ago; wherefore he practises in the Divorce Court; which is part of the Admiralty Division. He has been doing so for nearly thirty years; for more than twenty he has been inside the Bar; and for nearly twenty he has been a Bencher of the Inner Temple. He is also a Deputy-Lieutenant and a Justice of the Peace for Sussex; and he has been Mayor of Winchelsea (where he has a house) and Member of Parliament for Rye (where Winchelsea is). He is now not only the leader in the Divorce Court, but one of the many who owe their early successes to the patronage of that firm in Ely Place which is used to bring into Court the infidelities of the best known of the unfaithful. He did not always lead in the Divorce Court; but so soon as he took silk he displaced the learned ecclesiastical doctors of a bygone day who used to conduct the business of Divorce: for he is a man of infinite tact who has succeeded in getting the ear of Presidents so widely different as the staidly decorous Sir James Hannen, the nautically jovial Sir Charles Butt, and the fastidiously courteous Sir Francis Jeune. His manners are gentlemanly, very smiling, and exceedingly quiet; and, in spite of all that he has gone through, he still preserves the air of a dilettante. His voice is soft and so low that the Judge is often the only man who hears him; which is further evidence of his tact. He can skate very lightly over very thin ice; and he is a good, kindly fellow who is generally liked by his clients.

He has dabbled in history; he is said to be wealthy, and he is supposed to like comfort. Despite his forensic achievements, his domestic life is irreproachable.

**Mr. Andrew Graham Murray**
(1849–1942) Page 69
Andrew Graham Murray is the eldest son of the late Thomas Graham Murray, who was for some years Crown Agent for Scotland. He, being partner in Tods, Murray and Jamieson, the biggest firm of Writers to the Signet in Scotland, very naturally sent his son to the Scottish Bar, via Harrow and Cambridge. The son disappointed his friends at the former place by doing no work at the latter; but when he was called to the Scotch Bar at the mature age of twenty-five (which was two-and-twenty years ago), his own quick wit and his father's support made him known at once; while his ability as a cross-examiner, and the celerity with which he picked up the points of the most intricate case have since brought him to the top of the tree. He was a Queen's Counsel only five years ago; but he was appointed Solicitor-General when Lord Darling was put on the Bench; and last year he became Lord Advocate, in succession to Sir Charles Pearson. He has been Sheriff of Perthshire; and in Parliament he is the Conservative elect of Buteshire.

He is so fond of sport that he studies each of its branches as though it were an exact science; for he is a Scotchman. He is a good shot, a keen golfer, and a precise billiard player; but although he has driven a tandem up to the Parliament House, he has never been seen on the top of a horse. Yet he rides a bicycle. Being devoted to dancing, he goes out a great deal; and although he has a grown up family he can give most young men points as a keeper of late hours. He is, indeed, so hard that he can dance till five in the morning and come up smiling in Court before ten; while he has been known to leave a ball at two, get up a case, and be dancing again at four. He is very popular in the Parliament House; he has a good head, and his knowledge of Caledonian affairs is unplumbed. In the House of Commons he made his mark on the Scotch Land Bill; but being a Harrow boy he has sent his son to Eton. He is very unlike his father, and for a Scot, he is an exceedingly gay person.

He can mend a bicycle.

**The Hon. Sir James Stirling**
(1836–1916) Page 70
The sixty-year-old son of an Aberdeen minister, both his parentage and his innate sense of right ordained him for the clerical profession; but circumstances were too strong for predestination, and when he had learned a little at King's College (Aberdeen) he showed such mathematical bent that they sent him to Trinity (Cambridge): which College he honoured by becoming Senior Wrangler. That marked him as a man of exactitude; and being brother to a solicitor, he was naturally made a barrister, and very properly chose to practice on the Chancery side. His brother had many eminently respectable clients, and soon he was known as a good conveyancer, with a large equity practice. But large as it was he did all the work intrusted to him so well that he was presently appointed Treasury Junior on the Equity side: which, according to all precedent, meant that promotion to the Bench over the heads of the Inner Bar which in due course happened.

He has now been a Judge for ten years; staid, decorous, sound, and therefore colourless. He was nothing of an advocate; which makes him the better Judge. He is a good lawyer, very patient, very amiable, very painstaking, and always fair. On the other hand, he is careful to the verge of timidity; so that he is rarely persuaded to make an Order until he can find a reported case which he can follow as an authority. He is not so slow as Mr. Justice North, nor so talkative as Mr. Justice (now Lord Justice) Chitty; but he is sounder than Mr. Justice Kekewich. And so by the absence of judicial vices he is made judicially virtuous.

Altogether he is not a great Judge, nor a strong one, nor a bad one.

**The Hon. Sir John Compton Lawrance**
(1832–1912) Page 71
His father was the late Thomas Munton Lawrance, of Dunsby Hall, Lincolnshire, and his mother was a daughter of the late John Compton, of Water Newton, Wansford; and from them four-and-sixty years ago he took his names. Twenty-seven years later he was a barrister; and at forty-five he was a Queen's Counsel. Then he tried to get into Parliament for Peterborough; and though he failed to do so, he was made Recorder of Derby. A year later Conservatives of South Lincolnshire returned him; and five years later the Stamford Division chose him. Yet another five years and he was put above Parliament by being raised to the Bench: which was a very proper reward for his services, and not undeserved.

He has now done seven years as a Judge of the Queen's Bench; yet has he not served his full time. When, as a Lincolnshire country gentleman, he found his way to the Bar, he soon acquired a considerable practice before country juries; for not only did they know him, but he knew them—thoroughly. When he took silk, he did still better; for he had no formidable rival on the Midland Circuit. His appointment as a Judge provoked considerable criticism; but he has since shown (not for the first time) that a gentleman who knows his own mind, keeps his temper, and acts with absolute impartiality, may make a very satisfactory Judge, even though he may not be a profound lawyer. And, indeed, although Counsel like him, he is not at all a bad Judge. Nevertheless his success, both at the bar and in the world, is rather due to the personal liking of people for a hearty, cheerful, long and large country gentleman than to any legal attribute of which he may be possessed.

He is a good average Judge and a good plain man. He is known as "Long Lawrance."

**Mr. Henry Fielding Dickens, Q.C.**
(1849–1933) Page 72
The fifth surviving son of the Inventor of Pickwick, he was born seven-and-forty years ago; and, having been made a Bachelor of Arts, he was called to the Bar by the Honourable Society of the Inner Temple. He began to practice in the South-Eastern Counties, where his father's name was one to conjure with; and finding, in the fulness of time, that Kent and Sussex were growing tired of Mr. Willis, he ventured to take silk. The venture was wise; for he has since gotten a substantial and steadily increasing practice as a leader. He has been Recorder of Deal, and he is now Recorder of Maidstone; which is in the very center of the county of Pickwick. He is a very painstaking, cheerful advocate; yet with all his merit he owes a good deal to the fact that he is the son of a popular idol.

He is an industrious and pleasant gentleman who has no particular history at the Bar.

**The Honourable Francis Henry Bacon**
(b. 1832) Page 73
He is the son of the late Vice-Chancellor Bacon, that able Real Property Lawyer whom he greatly resembles in person if not in knowledge; and he was born nearly sixty years ago. He was called to the Bar by the Honourable Society of Lincoln's Inn one-and-forty years since; and having travelled the Eastern Circuit more or less successfully for two decades, he was shelved as Judge of the Bloomsbury County Court Circuit No. 42, and a year later of the Whitechapel County Court Circuit No. 39. As a Bloomsbury Judge, Regent Street and the neighbourhood are within his jurisdiction; and although he is a bachelor he has acquired much knowledge of female attire; chiefly gained by adjudicating between dressmakers and their victims. For it is his humour in disputes between these classes to make the client put on the dressmaker's work in the privacy of the Judge's room; after which his Honour enters, and, like Solomon, pronounces judgement on the fit: generally in favour of the fitter. As a Whitechapel Judge he has acquired much knowledge of the lower kind of Hebrew; whom he detests, as the Jew abhors him and his name. He has indeed, a keen scent for humbug, which he has whetted on the foreign Israelite. Nevertheless he is a man of character if not without foibles: and he inherits some of his great father's shrewdness with more of his humour. With all his faults of testiness, rudeness, and alleged unfairness—alleged, of course, by unsuccessful litigants—he is, on the whole, a good Judge; who holds very decided views as to the dignity of his Office.

He is no respecter of persons, but a capital after-dinner speaker.

**Sir Mancherjee Merwanjee Bhownaggree, K.C.I.E., M.P.**
(1851–1933) Page 74
The late Merwanjee N. Bhownaggree, Bombay merchant, and his wife Cooverbai, became his parents six-and-forty years ago; and they gave him educational chance, of which he took all advantage, at Bombay University and at Elphinstone College in the same Presidency. That fitted him for London and Lincoln's Inn: where twelve years since he was made a Barrister. He then proceeded to show the stuff that was in him: as a journalist, as head of the Bhaunagar State Agency, as Judicial Councillor, as Commissioner of Kathiawar State at the Colonial and Indian Exhibition, and in diverse other ways. He is a Justice of the Peace for Bombay, the author of such works as "The Constitution of the East India Company," and a Conservative who two years ago beat Mr. George Howell for the North-East Division of Bethnal Green. He has already made his mark in Parliament—if only as an extinguisher for Sir William Wedderburn. Outside the House he has devoted himself to the education of women—especially amongst the Parsees in Western India.

He is an admirable type of that ancient Zoroastrian Persian race which was some years ago described (by one Herodotus) as energetic, courageous, magnanimous, intellectual, and quick; and to these qualities he attributes his political success thus far. If, being warned by its history, he can overcome the faults of his race—pugnacity, rashness, and obstinacy—if he will discipline himself to serious and steady work, he has a real English future before him; for he has many good qualities. He is a cheerful fellow, fond of repartee; who loves poetry, and enjoys society.

He is a good-natured, modest, rather vain, careful

legislator, who was worthily improved into a Knight Companion of the Indian Empire on his Queen-Empress's Diamond Jubilee Day.

**Mr. Justice John Charles Bigham**
**Viscount Mersey**
(1840–1929) Page 75

John Charles Bigham was born to a Liverpool merchant seven-and-fifty years ago; and having begun his education at the Royal Institution, Liverpool, he continued it in Paris and Berlin, carried it on as a business man in Liverpool, and completed it at the Bar: whither he was called at the age of thirty by the Honourable Society of the Middle Temple. He joined the Northern Circuit and soon began to base his success at the Bar upon the foundation of his business knowledge: which was partly inherited and partly acquired. Thirteen years after his call he took silk; another two years and he was an unsuccessful candidate for the East Toxteth Division of Liverpool; yet another year and he was a Bencher of his Inn; in 1892 he was again beaten for the Exchange Division of his own place; and a little more than two years ago he tried again and went into Parliament. And now he is one of the newest and shrewdest Judges of the High Court of Justice.

As a Counsel he had the advantage of a private income, much industry, and considerable ability; so that he rapidly rose in his profession. Remarkable more for his versatility than any other particular quality, nothing came amiss to him; and he soon showed himself a capable advocate, a painstaking lawyer, and a weighty arguer of legal points. Presently he was recognised as an excellent commercial lawyer, an expert in bankruptcy law, and an effective cross-examiner—especially of a co-respondent; while he could hold his own in any Court against any leader of the Bar. His admirers have described him as the best all-round man of his time; and though he was never a Russell as an advocate nor a Webster as a weight-carrier, he could generally stand up to either. As a Counsel he was known for his trick of gravely saying to a contradictory witness, "Well, we shall see!" As a Judge he is full of the promise of a man who ought to make his mark; and his only fault seems to be that, like most strong men dressed in authority, he has not yet learned that patience is a virtue. He gets through as much work in a day as most Judges; he is a good-tempered little fellow who has a sense of humour, and he possesses quite an adequate idea of his own importance.

He made himself at home his first day on the Bench; and as to his future, well—we shall see.

**The Hon. Mr. Justice Sir Arthur Moseley Channell**
(1838–1928) Page 76

The Honourable Sir Arthur Moseley Channell, now one of the puisne Judges in the Queen's Bench Division, began life precisely sixty years ago as son of the late Sir William Fry Channell, Baron of the Exchequer: so that he is of quite legal parentage. From the nursery he went to Harrow; then to Trinity, Cambridge (where he first became known as a Wrangler); and thence to the Bar, by way of the Inner Temple. He practised as a Junior for two-and-twenty years, and as a Leader for twelve. He has been Recorder for Rochester, and Vice-Chairman of the General Council of the Bar. He has also been twice married, and he is now a Knight.

As a Junior, his practice was very general; as a "silk," he chiefly conducted cases without juries, and very frequently argued points of Local Government Law before the Court in banc. He has, indeed, made himself an authority on such small matters as pertain to vestries, boards, sewers, waterworks, and new streets. He was never a great lawyer, nor an eloquent advocate; but he is well known as a good "workman," with considerable knowledge of the Law and its Practice; and though never expected to be brilliant, he could always be trusted to make no mistakes. It may be said of him that during all his four-and-thirty years of practice he never made an enemy among his brethren, his clients, or his opponents; and it is certain that he never received anything but friendly attention from the Bench. He is a quiet, kindly, considerate gentleman, quite free from conceit; in whose keeping the wholesome traditions of the English Bench for good sense in civil matters and for humanity in criminal will be quite safe.

He will not make a great Judge; but he is a very worthy sitter in the high place which he has honourably attained by long service to the Law.

**Sir John George Witt, Q.C.**
(1837–1906) Page 77

He is sixty-one years old, a Cambridge man, a Bencher of Lincoln's Inn, and a jocular, loud-voiced person who yet occupies a position. He is also a long, lean advocate who has considerable knowledge of the Stock Exchange, of the ways of the City man, of the racecourse, and of a horse. And he knows something of the rig of a ship. Personally, he is a good-natured fellow whose sporting air makes him look so little of the Queen's Counsel that it comes as a shock to learn that he was once a Don (and Senior Fellow) of King's. Professionally, however, he has long enjoyed, both as junior and as leader, the confidence of solicitors who like a man of the world to their Counsel. He knows, indeed, most of the wicked ways of man, and he is as well able to take care of his clients as of himself.

He has not a very refined manner; but he is a much better lawyer than he looks.

**Mr. William Otto Adolph Julius Danckwerts**
(1853–1914) Page 78

William Otto Adolph Julius Danckwerts is a rude and learned personage who is becoming quite celebrated at the Bar. By parentage a Boer, he shows some of the well-known characteristics of his race; for he is a pushing, hard-working fellow, with an acute, if ponderous, intellect. He was called just twenty years ago; and having found his way into chambers that were the nursery of a succession of Treasury "devils" in the persons of such eminent Judges as the late Lord Justice Bowen, Mr. Justice A.L. Smith, and Mr. Justice R.S. Wright, he had to console himself in the Office of Treasury Counsel to the Commissioners of Inland Revenue. He enjoys quite a large practice which is as solid as himself; and this may partly account for the fact that he is not the most popular of his professional brethren: who cannot be brought to like his brusque want of manners. When he differs from an opponent he is quite ready to tell him that his conduct is "disgraceful"; and the criticism is generally resented by the novice, though he soon learns that this is merely a Boer way of paying a compliment to an adversary. His abuse, indeed, is to be taken in a Pickwickian sense; and, due allowance being made for his shortcomings, he is not at all a bad fellow.

He has fairly earned a very good position by distinguished ability. He has also married a handsome wife who belongs to an old English family.

**Mr. Henry Bargrave Finnelly Deane, Q.C.**
(1846–1919) Page 79

Son of the leader of the Probate and Divorce Division of the High Court, he naturally went thither so soon as he was called; and he is now an example of success at the Bar by patience and industry. For he made but little way during many years: Inderwick, Searle, and Bayford taking practically all the junior work; and the two latter taking it after the first took silk. So for long he tried the Common Law and the South-Eastern Circuit; and never relaxing his connection with the President's Court he learned his business thoroughly. He became known in the Court in which he is now a leader some fifteen years after his call to the Bar; and when Sir Francis Jeune became President, his success was assured: for that Judge both realised the force of his arguments and perceived the sense of his observations. On his part he realised his success, and after ten years of heavy practice took silk: so that now he shares with Mr. Inderwick the leadership of that Court which is presided over by the Great Unmarrier; while his old friend and rival Mr. Bayford has decided to retire into country life.

He is quite an able, good-natured, hard-working advocate who, if he have no genius, had much tact and very complete knowledge of his trade. He has a face of peculiar solemnity, and, when waxing eloquent, he can assume the air of grief so profound that he really seems about to weep under its encumbrance. He may be laughing behind the mask: but if so he does not permit many of us to penetrate it; and so he carries much weight. He is a keen Volunteer, and once a Captain of the Finsbury Rifles he is now Colonel of the "Devil's Own." He is Wykehamist and a Balliol Master of Arts, who was born rather more than half a century ago, took an International Law Prize for an Essay at Oxford, was made Official Principal of the Archdeaconries of Rochester and St. Albans, and despite the nastinesses in which he is constantly involved he looks younger than he is. He will presently retire to a Scottish moor for the proper purpose.

He once wrote a Treatise on "The Law of Blockade." He survives it.

**The Hon. Sir Walter George Frank Phillimore, Bart., D.C.L.**
**Baron Phillimore**
(1845–1929) Page 80

It is useful for a barrister of eminence to have been born to a Judge; if only because a Lord Chancellor, when beset by newspaper criticism until he is in doubt whither he shall turn to fill a judicial gap, is able to select him as being of the Judicial caste. When Mr. Justice Channell had been selected, amid general applause, to succeed his father on the Bench, the Lord Chancellor played the same card again with the son of the late Judge of the Admiralty Court. But Sir Walter Phillimore had more virtues than that of an honoured name: he was himself a learned, honourable, and courteous gentleman who had long had a fine practice in the Courts of Admiralty. Accordingly he was chosen to preside over a Common Law Court, before which no Admiralty case can come: which was something of a surprise; for an alleged ignorance of the Common Law is only excusable in a Judge when he has been a politician, or has done service to his Party. Now, Sir Walter was—a Judge has no politics—a philosophic and philanthropic Radical of the ancient type: who, having thrice attempted to win Conservative seats, has won a judicial one—without even taking "silk."

He is the second Baronet; he is a Westminster boy and a Christ Church man, and he is three-and-fifty. He has also been a Fellow of All Souls, and he is an Oxfordshire magistrate. He belongs to Henley, he is a Bencher and a husband, and, though he was only made a Judge last year, he has shown himself so firm, so polite, and so painstaking as to have justified the Lord Chancellor in his selection. More than this, he has surprised the Bar by his unknown acquaintance with the Common Law of England: which is only less than that of one or two of his older brethren. It is not too much to say that before he had sat into his third term he was recognised as one of the best of our puisne Judges. Personally he is a very amiable man who takes very serious views of life. He is also a pronounced High Churchman who so greatly objects to divorce (on principle) that, as a Counsel, he declined to practice in the Divorce Court; although it is believed that he once appeared for the Queen's Proctor. He has, indeed, dared to state from the Bench his objections to making decrees nisi absolute as Vacation Judge; though he has too much respect for the President to decline to do as his predecessors have done before him. Finally, it may be added that he has enterprise; for when he failed to obtain "silk" he took out a patent of precedence, and walked within the Bar without the Lord Chancellor's leave.

Altogether he is an ornament to his profession, who has deserved his success.

**Mr. Franklin Lushington**
(1823–1907) Page 81

Sir John Bridge, the excellent Chief Magistrate of the Metropolis, has this week retired from the important position that he has held so well for so long; and promoted in his stead is Mr. Franklin Lushington, an elderly gentleman, who is actually his predecessor's senior, both as a man and as a London Stipendiary Magistrate. For Mr. Lushington became the fourth son of a puisne Judge of Ceylon no fewer than six-and-seventy years ago; so that his beginning is now a matter of ancient history. Nevertheless, it is on record that he began well at Rugby and at Trinity, Cambridge; where he was Senior Classic and First Chancellor's Medallist. Then, being his father's son, he went to the Bar, and presently became a Member of the Supreme Council of Justice in the Ionian Islands. He was there for three years: but he is still a

Justice of the Peace for five English counties; and having been a Police Magistrate for thirty dull years, he is to-day at the top of the magisterial tree: as a reward, presumably, for long service. It is a pity that the Chief Magistrate of London should not be a younger man; for, though he is a kindly soul and a gentlemanly president in his Court, he is not always alive to distinctions between the common policeman and the passing witness who is without interest in the case: for he believes in the Police. He is a creature of routine; who gets through his work without great speed, but with considerable punctuality. He is the inferior of his predecessor in strength, if not in urbanity; and his manner is at once less judicial and less tactful. But comparisons being invidious, it is enough to add that he is a very kindly and attentive man—especially to the Police.

### Mr. Justice Henry Burton Buckley

(1845–1935) Page 82

Henry Burton Buckley became the fourth son of a late Vicar of St. Mary's, Paddington, five-and-fifty years ago; after which he was sent to Merchant Taylors' School, where they converted him into a scholar of Christ's College, Cambridge. There, in due course, he graduated so well that he was Fellow. Thirty years ago he was called to the Bar, and while quite a young man he wrote a book on Company Law which may be described as a classic; insomuch as it ranks with Lindley on Partnership as a text-book for the profession. That great book brought Mr. Buckley into practice, then to silk, and, lastly, to the Bench; most worthily. He is a cold, able, hard-working Judge whose head is quite clear. He has unbounded capacity for work, yet he was never much of an advocate— except with Judges who recognised good law when they heard it expounded: and with them his words of wisdom carried weight. His manner is somewhat repellent; but he must have a soft spot somewhere in his nature, for after forty he wooed and won a very charming lady; and in due course (as a late Judge remarked at the time) found a new Memorandum of Association.

He is our newest Judge, he is very solemn, and he is doing well.

### Lord Chief Justice Richard Everard Webster
### Viscount Alverstone

(1842–1915) Page 83

Born as plain "Dick" Webster, and christened Richard Everard, he is the second son of a Queen's Counsel who has more than followed in his father's footsteps; for though he is but eight-and-fifty he has filled many great Offices, and is now Baron Alverstone, Lord Chief Justice of England. His career at the Bar is well known; and it is generally believed that he owes his success to considerable ability, tempered by painstaking industry, early rising, and regular attention to work. On the Bench he is less well known, since he was Master of the Rolls for but a few weeks before he came to the scarlet of the Lord Chief Justice; but he promises to make an admirable Judge. He is even-tempered, dignified, and affable; he is a really great lawyer with a clear mind and a lucid manner of expressing it, and if he be not so brilliant a man as his predecessor, his substantial merits are probably greater. His sternest critic can find no more fault in him than a little pompousness of manner; and all agree that he is an ornament to the Bench.

He has always been at once popular and respected; for he is a good fellow as well as a deserving. He was a scholar of Trinity, Cambridge, a thirty-fifth Wrangler, a third-class classic, and an athletic Blue; who has never since taken much interest in amateur athleticism. As Attorney-General he was so conscientious as to be able successfully to distinguish between himself as Counsel and as Crown Officer in the same case; and altogether he is a great lawyer, a very "straight" man, and a good friend.

He is the soul of Honour.

### Mr. Justice Gainsford Bruce

(1834–1912) Page 84

This judge of eight years' standing and six-and-sixty years of age is a Glasgow University man and a Durham Doctor of Civil Law, who began his career at the Bar forty years ago. He held various offices quite adequately, he helped to write a book on Admiralty Practice and another on Shipping, he was

in Parliament for a short time (after four repulses), and now, though the slowest, is far from being the least unworthy occupant of Her Majesty's Bench. He has attended four annual Assizes at Manchester and Liverpool, and is supposed to have given more satisfaction to the merchants of those northern towns than have many of his more brilliant and versatile brethren. He is a very careful, conscientious, hard-working Judge, who takes a long time to master the evidence and the law of the case; but having mastered them, he very seldom goes wrong in his judgement. He is also a severe Churchman, who has been nominated to exercise the jurisdiction of a judge under the Benefices' Act of 1898; yet he has been known to laugh. In the Admiralty Court he was once obliged to read an entry in the ship's log according to which the crew had found it "very slow work pushing the old Bruce along."

Although he is quite a good Judge, and those who know him affirm that he is not so depressing a companion as his cast of visage would seem to imply.

### The Hon. Mr. Justice Cozens-Hardy
### Baron Cozens-Hardy

(1838–1920) Page 85

It has already been said that by birth, by social position, and by education he is a Radical; for one-and-sixty years ago he became the son of Mr. William Cozens-Hardy, of Letheringsett, in Norfolk: who was a Liberal Justice of the Peace; and a few years later he began his education at Amersham, to continue it at University College, London, and at the feet of Mr. Gladstone. He is a Fellow of University College, a double graduate of London University, a member of the Reform Club, and a very excellent, absolutely honest Judge. He began to practice at the Bar forty years ago; and he took to Equity and Real Property Law so kindly that nine years later he was chosen to examine in those dry subjects on behalf of London University. Twenty years of quiet, painstaking practice brought him to silk, when he had long been known in Lincoln's Inn as one of the best of all the Juniors in Chancery. Then he became the only leader in Mr. Justice North's Court. At the Bar he was known for his integrity; being so very honest and so openly candid that the most suspicious Judge was never unready to put his trust in him; and withal he was a careful, precise, and hardworking student of Law. Although he knows something about patents, he was, as a Member of Parliament, able to swallow Home Rule; but now he has been an ornament of the Bench for nearly two years. Since Lord Justice Romer made room for him there, none finds fault with him.

He is not a vain man; yet is he as fair a Judge as he is uncomely.

### Lord Justice John Rigby

(1834–1903) Page 86

He was born seven-and-sixty years ago; and he began life at Liverpool College. Thence he went to Cambridge, and did some of that exact mathematical work which argues absence of imagination; becoming Second Wrangler and Smith's Prizeman, and a Fellow. Accordingly, he went to the Bar, and in due course was called within it and mastered his business, and was made a Bencher. He worked for the Treasury, and became a Member of Parliament, and a Solicitor-General and an Attorney-General; for his only vice (besides a dirty pipe and a certain eloquence of diction) was his vain Radicalism: which was partly compensated for by the friendship of the late Mr. Gladstone; who believed in him. And so he was elevated to the Bench of the Court of Appeal seven years ago: after much rivalry between the polite Sir Horace Davey and the unpolished Sir John Rigby. He is known for his solid honesty, his robust manner, and his high idea of his Office; and if he have not turned out to be quite so great a Judge as was anticipated, that may be due to the fact that his health is not quite so good as it was when he took the floor in the House of Commons. He cares for nobody, being strong in his own sense of independence; and though his temper is gusty he has a host of friends. Like many other eminent Chancery men, he has not very much history; but he is, nevertheless, a sturdy, good, honest fellow, who believes in himself.

In summer, he patronises the penny steamer; and he has been known to ride a horse eloquently.

### Sir Frederick Albert Bosanquet
### Common Law Serjeant of London

(1837–1923) Page 87

Frederick Albert Bosanquet was born to a Welshman four-and-sixty years ago. From the Principality he came to Eton and King's College, Cambridge; where he was a Classical First, a Senior Optime, and a Fellow. Then he joined the Inner Temple, and for years was a familiar feature of the Oxford Circuit; until after some twenty years of more or less consistent practice—as Junior Counsel to the Admiralty and other things—he took silk. He also wrote a treatise on "The Statutes of Limitation" and Recorded for Worcester and Wolverhampton until last year, when he was improved into Common Serjeant. He stood once for Parliament, but the Election was over before he had time to state his case to the Electors; yet as a barrister he was always in great demand as an arbitrator. He was, indeed, an admirable lawyer, if rather too slow and solemn to be a very successful advocate in any but the most ponderous cases. On circuit his portentous solemnity of manner earned him a reputation for wit; but another member of it once said (perhaps in jealousy) that the Oxford Circuit could not recognise wit when they met with it. Now he is quite a good Judge in the Mayor's Court and at the Old Bailey; for he is one of those men who do better as a Judge than as an advocate.

### Mr. John Gordon Swift MacNeill, K.C., M.P.

(1849–1926) Page 88

He is a parson's son of three-and-fifty who ought to know better; but if he does not always behave as an Irish gentleman should, he is an Irish barrister who claims relationship with the late Dean Swift. He has taken classical honours at Trinity College, Dublin, and at Christ Church, Oxford, and he obstructs legislation on behalf of South Donegal in the unfortunate House of Commons, while he professes Constitutional and Criminal Law in King's Inns. He is an extreme Home Ruler who, although he was believed to be attached to the Tim Healyite faction, is at home in the zareba of John Redmond without ever being antagonistic to Mr. Dillon. He has probably been called to order by the Speaker more often than any other Irishman; for he is politically full of insignificant sound and fury. He is also a pro-Boer who yet had many friends in the House until Monday last: when by applauding the painful news of a national disaster he succeeded in overstepping the limits of bad taste.

### Mr. Charles Alfred Cripps, K.C., M.P.

(1852–1941) Page 89

From his father, who was a Queen's Counsel, he inherited a reputation as an ecclesiastical lawyer just half a century ago; and now he is Vicar-General of both Provinces. But between his birth and his Vicar-Generalship many things happened. He learned manners and other matters at Winchester; whence, of course, he went to New College. He took four First Classes, and was made a Fellow of St. John's. Thence he went to the Parliamentary Bar, and made a hundred thousand guineas in ten years; after which he attempted to escape further worry from solicitors by going into the House itself (where he has represented the Stroud Division of Gloucestershire, and now represents the Stretford Division of Lancashire; where the electors are held to be shrewd folk). Yet is he still pursued with briefs marked with big fees for arbitration and railway and patent cases. He was also Attorney-General to the last Prince of Wales, and is in the same relation to the present Prince of Wales, besides being such other things as Deputy-Chairman of Quarter Sessions in Buckinghamshire and the author of a book on "The Law of Compensation" and another on Clergy Law. He wears an air of boyish and somewhat indolent affability; and although he is popular, he has quite a good opinion of himself.

He is just what he looks—a very amiable fellow.

### The Hon. Sir Joseph Walton

(1845–1910) Page 90

He went to the Bar four-and-thirty years ago, being then twenty-three, and it is just ten years since he was called within the Bar. As a junior he worked at Liverpool; so well that he soon acquired the leading practice, and with it a good knowledge of commercial law and commercial men. Then he came to town and acquired the leading practice in the Commercial Court; and being a good lawyer and a good fellow, he came to the Bench with unusual credit among his brethren. As a Judge he is as sound as ever, even if he be a little slow; especially with juries. He will, indeed, be more useful when he is gone up to the Court of Appeal; but he is quite a good-tempered fellow without airs or affectations, who is well liked in his profession.

He has an agreeable smile, and he is a Roman Catholic.

**Sir Edward George Clarke, K.C.**
(1841–1931) Page 91
Born two-and-sixty years ago, he has since filled many parts, and is now the head of the unofficial Bar of England. Of humble origin (his father was a jeweller in King William Street), he has never been ashamed of it, but rather proud of the dignity which himself has undoubtedly won by sheer ability and merit. Educated at Edmonton and the City Commercial School, at the City of London College and at King's College Evening Classes, he has done them all credit, and is now a Fellow of King's College, London. At eighteen he was a writer in the India Office; yet found time (and ability) to become Tancred Law Student a couple of years later. That drove him to the Bar. He was in the Penge case a quarter of a century ago, and Southwark sent him to Parliament for a month or two. Then he went to Plymouth, and represented that wholesome place for ten years. He was in the Bartlett case, and was improved into Solicitor-General. His other and more recent cases are legion; so that he is something like a public idol, though his appearance is less attractive than his wonderful personality. He owes his position to the fact that, besides being a very adroit advocate, he is, when occasion demands, a genuinely eloquent speaker; for, however ready a speaker the barrister is, he is seldom really eloquent. On several public occasions, indeed, Sir Edward has made speeches full of real feeling and real wit in which you could find no word out of place; for the speeches were models of English eloquence. In the House of Commons he has been no less successful than on the platform, and it is something of a mystery to the uninitiated that he has not found his way to very high Office; for it is known that he has declined high judicial position. It may be said of him, indeed, that had he managed his own career as well as he has managed the cases of his clients he would have achieved all the public eminence that he could desire.

But he holds his own independent views on every subject; and these have not always been the views of his Party.

**Alexander Burns Shand, P.C., D.C.L., LL.D.**
**Baron Shand**
(1828–1904) Page 92
Alexander Burns Shand, P.C., D.C.L., LL.D., son of Alexander Shand of Aberdeen, is five-and-seventy years old, the holder of a Peerage created eleven years ago, a vara wee man, and vara Scotch. His education was varied, for it was achieved at Glasgow, Edinburgh and Heidelberg; yet he still talks Scotch. He is an Honorary Graduate of Oxford University, and Honorary Bencher of Gray's Inn, and a member of the Athenæum Club; while he has been Sheriff of Kincardineshire, of Haddington, and of Berwick; a Judge of the Court Session (where one learns real wit); a Deputy-Lieutenant of Edinburgh City; a Commissioner under the Educational Endowments Act for Scotland, and many other wholesome Scottish things: besides which he was well nominated Chairman of the Coal Industry Conciliation Board some nine years ago. Scots Law is popularly believed to be a thing which only a great intellect can master; but Lord Shand has mastered as much of that erudition as any one man has ever been known to master. That is why he was promoted from the Scottish Bench to be a supernumerary Law Lord and his promotion was received by the profession with general approval. And so, having all his life through been devoted to golf, he now plays the game in company with the Lord Chancellor or the Speaker; and he has even been known to play with the Prime Minister. Although he is not a long driver, he is so beloved of golfers that on one well-known links a bunker is named after him simply because he has been seen in it so often.

Nevertheless, his wee body supports a head that is chock full of legal lore tempered by much acumen.

**Mr. Edward Marshall Hall, K.C., M.P.**
(1858–1929) Page 93
Born at Brighton five-and-forty years ago, they sent him to Rugby and Cambridge and the Inner Temple; of which he is now an ornament. He practised on the South-Eastern Circuit, took silk at forty, and won the Southport Division of Lancashire from his liberal predecessor at the last General Election. He is a good fellow, who is gifted with a dash of rousing eloquence which, though it may be more impressive than logical, puts him in great favour with those litigants whose best chance of winning a case is to convey an unfavourable impression of the opposing party; so that he is a really strong Counsel in what is called a "losing case." In the Criminal Courts he is so clever a defender of prisoners he is supposed to have restored quite a number of burglars to their friends and relations. He may not be a great lawyer, but he is a good advocate, who has always successfully weathered the judicial storms that his ready speech has brought upon his head; and he seems likely to weather many more of them. For he has a very taking way with him, and although some of those who know him regard him as aggressive, he is naturally a kind-hearted, rather nervous fellow, who hides his modesty under a bushel of assertiveness. In private life he is so keen a collector of old silver, miniatures, and other curios that he would readily devote all his time to the dear labour of adding to his really fine museum of these things. He is a capital host, who can tell a good story; he is a golfer, a racquet player, and a good shot; he has many friends, and quite a distinguished appearance.

The British jury believes in him, and the British public admires him; but Lord Justice Mathew is supposed not to love him.

**Mr. Robert Alfred McCall, K.C.**
(1849–1934) Page 94
It is fifty-seven years since he became an Irishman at Lisburn, and the third son of a well-known Ulster journalist. But he went to Queen's College in Belfast, and in Galway; and so, avoiding his father's profession, he came easily to the Middle Temple, of which he [is] now a Bencher. Yet he still plays golf, rides a bicycle, and occasionally hits indiarubber balls over a net. At the Bar he made a reputation as a junior by his strong readiness to "fight" a case, and though his combativeness is now tempered, he can still stand to his guns with a dogged pertinacity that pleases many clients. He can also call a spade by its proper name; though at home he is a kindly, genial host, racy of the soil of Ulster.

He has a place at Walmer, and he has been Captain of the Cinque Ports Golf Club.

**Mr. Rufus Daniel Isaacs, K.C.**
**Marquess of Reading**
(1860–1935) Page 95
His father, a merchant in the City of London, gave him a good education at University College School, and he became a man of the world by acquiring larger knowledge in Brussels and in Hanover. He is only four-and-forty, but he is full of brains, and he has seen a good deal of life. It is said that he first went to sea; but presently he returned, to business, and he has never been "at sea" since. His abilities, however, were too great for ordinary business, so he tried the Stock Exchange, and found that its walls limited his ambitions. Finally he learned his true vocation as an Advocate; for he is now at the top of his profession, having gained the dizzy eminence at a very early age by sheer hard work and real merit. For he has the unusual combination of great brain power with invincible endurance; for in his younger days he was an adept at boxing, while he still keeps himself "fit" by riding, cycling, and golfing. Thus he is still well able to take a great deal of physical as well as legal beating; being one of those who never give in while he has a leg left to stand upon. He is naturally at his best in a commercial, or Stock Exchange case; for of such he knows all the ropes. Nevertheless his fame brings him big briefs in sensational and fashionable cases of all kinds; in which he makes no mistakes. He does not try to be brilliant; he has a quiet and very convincing way with him, and altogether, with the single exception of Sir Edward Clarke, he is recognised as the leader of the Common Law Bar.

Socially, he is quite popular; for not only is he exceedingly clever, rather good-looking, and very good-tempered, but he is absolutely devoid of conceit.

**The Hon. Sir Arthur Richard Jelf, K.C.**
(1837–1917) Page 96
Genial, urbane, and humorous, rejoicing through life Jelf goes. Even the prisoner at the bar can awake his humour and evoke his sympathy. One such, awaiting sentence, at heart a hypocrite, shed copious tears to soften the heart of the Recorder of Shrewsbury. Now, this most wise and learned Judge as named Arthur Richard Jelf. "Why do you weep?" he asked. "Oh, my Lord, my dear Lord, I have never, never been in prison before." "Don't cry, prisoner at the bar," was the cheerful rejoinder, "I am going to send you there now." Mr. Justice Jelf was Recorder of Shrewsbury from 1879 to 1901.

It was only by chance that Dr. Jelf, Fellow of Oriel College, Oxford, for forty years Canon of Christ Church, and for twenty-four years Principal of King's College, London, was sent to Hanover to be tutor to George, its King, the blind son of the Duke of Cumberland. Lloyd, Regius Professor of Oxford, had sent for Newman, also a tutor at Oriel, and had offered him the post. "But how old are you?" said Lloyd. "Twenty-five," was the reply. "Go away, you are no use," was the curt retort. Lloyd had been entrusted to engage a tutor for this German Monarch and twenty-seven was the lowest age. Jelf, being two years older, was given the job. He went, he saw Emmy, Countess Schlippenbach of Prussia, a Maid of Honour to the Queen, and he conquered. The Prussian Countess became the wife of the Oriel tutor, and bore to him three sons.

The eldest son of this Jelf Trinity bore the Royal name of George, and in the fulness of time became Vicar of Blackheath and Canon of Rochester Cathedral. On the second his father's name was bestowed. Arthur Jelf having won untold popularity at the Bar, and a certain amount of filthy lucre, was given the ermine to which his urbanity has added a new charm. The youngest son was General Jelf. Passing through the "Shop," and having equal brains with his brothers, he became a Sapper, and now is again at the "Shop," this time as its head.

Jelf, the Judge, ought to be smothered by the halfpenny papers. He was educated at Eton and Christ Church, which all of us who read the halfpenny papers—and who doesn't?—know is the worst equipment for a young man with his way to make in the world. Yet in spite of this crushing weight, and without abstracting a single lead from the lead-cloth, for he always moulded his conduct in strict accordance with the splendid traditions of those ancient and aristocratic seats of learning, he has risen to the head of his profession, and in rising, has carried with him the good wishes and good will of every inhabitant of Temple and Inn.

Jelf is a thoroughly good fellow. No man has worked harder in his time than he has done. His manners are delightful; the charm of his personality cannot be excelled. He is the best of fathers, and lives in a delightful house at Putney. In election cases he was pre-eminent, and could in the execution of duty be really disagreeably severe to the man in the witness-box who was not on his side. He is fond of Scotland and takes exercise on Wimbledon Common. May Arthur Jelf long adorn the Bench to which he would have risen sooner had he not indulged in that most expensive luxury which, in ordinary parlance, is termed modesty!

**Sir Horace Edmund Avory, K.C.**
(1851–1935) Page 97
Horace Avory could have been nothing but a criminal lawyer. He tramps the boards of the Old Bailey as by hereditary right. For was not his father Clerk of Arraigns in that gloomy temple of justice, and is not his brother now holding the same position? Legend has it that his nurse, as she tied on his baby's cap, foresaw his future legal eminence in the infantile

gravity of his demeanour, a gravity that was eminently judicial. As a schoolboy he argued points in the rules of cricket and football with extreme logic. At Cambridge his efforts on the river, where he was captain of his college boat, disturbed his legal reflections; but once free from University trammels, he plunged into his hereditary profession with hereditary zeal.

He rose with persistent success. In 1875 he was called to the Bar; fourteen years later, when a mere child of thirty-eight, he became Junior Counsel for the Treasury. Ten years later he succeeded Mr. Gill as Senior Counsel for the same august body. There is no greater authority on crime than he, but he is no orator, as others are. Those fervid flights of eloquence that excite the jury and promote insomnia amongst Judges are not for him. He is, as a celebrated criminal once said of him, "a pertinacious beggar." That is where his strength lies, and it is for this reason that people who work in darkness by the aid of bull's-eye lanterns, equally with the fur-coated pioneers of fraud, regard him with regret and apprehension when he is for the Crown—and with joy and thanksgiving when he rises in their defence. To mention each *cause célèbre* in which he has appeared would be to relate the most famous trials of the last twenty years. In the days when the Sheriffs of London established a fund for the defence of criminals too poor to employ counsel, he was regularly retained by them. It is therefore no exaggeration to say that he has defended more murderers than any man living. The Liberator frauds, the Jameson Raiders, Lynch, and Whitaker Wright, are amongst the well-known cases that filled the newspapers with columns of reports and gave a fresh step up the ladder to Horace Avory.

He is not a maker of epigrams. Several of the stories concerning him circulated by junior members of the Bar he strenuously denies. But on one occasion he flashed out a retort that has remained in the minds of those who heard it. The counsel opposed to him quoted a text from the Book of Job to emphasise a point. "I do not think that such evidence is admissible," said Mr. Avory, with becoming gravity, "seeing that you cannot put Job in the witness-box."

He is a clean-shaven, wiry man. Over fifty he yet looks under forty. A good shot, a keen huntsman with the Surrey Union Foxhounds, a golfer, and a tennis player—in such recreations does he forget the atmosphere of the criminal courts. He also plays billiards, but with indifferent success. The United University and Garrick are his clubs. He is an authority on rating, and the legal mainstay of the L.C.C. Clever, shrewd, slim, he is bound to be a Judge—some day.

**The Rt. Hon. Herbert Henry Asquith, M.P.**
**Earl of Oxford and Asquith**
(1852–1928) Page 98
Manners makyth man, but brains made Herbert Henry Asquith. He has developed them by use, just as Sandow increases his biceps, and they have lifted him into a Cabinet.

Young Henry Asquith had as unpromising a start for a great political career as a lady novelist ever imagined for her hero. We first see him, a dour little lad, newly from Yorkshire, plodding away at the City of London School. Behind him was neither birth, nor wealth, nor influence. He was alone with his brains, and excellent comrades they were. From school he progressed as a Scholar to Balliol. He was never a very human undergraduate. There were some who, referring to his powers of application, called him a "smug." It was rude of them, but it was so. He became acquainted with Jowett, and acquired the Oxford manner and a first in "Mods." From that time nothing could hold him. He took the "Craven," and a first in "Greats." They made him a fellow of his college, and yet he was not contented. At the Union, of which he was president, he spoke ably and often. Curiously enough, his successes were followed almost step for step by his eldest son Raymond twenty-seven years later.

Henry Asquith attacked the Metropolis with ardour. While he read for the Bar, he worked as assistant master at his old school for two years. He was called, and began to take briefs. He still spoke when he could, and the Y.M.C.A. of Islington wondered at his eloquence. They thought his views rather broad, as all good Y.M.C.A.'s should; but he refused to change them.

Ten years later he had made a name, and was the chosen of East Fife. He entered the House with reserve in his eye and ambition in his soul. He was a solemn, untidy man. "I don't know if the honourable Member is a Nonconformist, but he looks like one," an opponent called across the floor of the House—rather rudely, it must be admitted. But the remark is illuminating. The chosen of East Fife began to grow in public opinion. His defence of Parnell in the Parnell Commission was brilliant. He is said to have kept Mr. Gladstone awake during the whole of an Eighty Club dinner. Obviously he was bound to rise.

In 1892 Mr. Gladstone gave him the moving of the resolution which brought to an end the Government of Lord Salisbury. He hit out almost with the vigour of a Chamberlain, and the G.O.M. made him Home Secretary, amidst the enthusiastic applause of those who had not expected the billet themselves. He was, on the whole, a success. He stood no nonsense from the Fenians, and they hung him in effigy. There were few murderers reprieved in his consulship. Judicious, sound, law-abiding—such is his record. In '95 he was out again, and back to the Bar, a more benignant figure, with longer hair than of old.

In '94 all London came to his second marriage, with Miss Margaret Tennant. They had both been members of the select society, the "Souls." Miss Margaret Tennant chose him from several candidates. "I understand he was the only man who could ask with success," remarked a noble jester on hearing of the match.

Beneath the fence on which Sir H.C.B. sits with the Radical Leadership dangling in his fingers, waits Henry Asquith, looking upward. After his marriage there were Radicals who thought he had grown to love society too dearly to be the same politician as of yore. His work in the House has interfered with his work in the Law Courts—also the contrary holds good. His effort to think Imperially in the shade of Lord Rosebery has damaged him with the Little England brigade. His Oxford manner has not endeared him to others. But though he will never arouse enthusiasm and devotion in his followers, he will be the Leader of his party.

There is an amusing little story of a passage of arms in the Law Courts between the political K.C. and Sir Edward Clarke. Voice lozenges were the subject of the case, and upon their medicinal value Mr. Asquith had spread himself with becoming eloquence. "Is there not such a thing as cacoëthes loquendi—a disease of speaking?" smiled the Judge. "Yes, my Lord," said Sir Edward. "My learned friend and I both suffer from it."

As a speaker he is terse, epigrammatic, sarcastic. His impromptus are best when prepared. He prefers to follow, rather than precede, events. He is unequalled in getting up a political case. Of the few oratorical slips recorded of him, is a Cambridge speech, in which he declared in a loud-voiced peroration, that of his party's demands he would abate "not one jit or one tottle." He once rode a cycle of his own make. He has taken to a frock coat since his marriage, and drives a pair of ponies with caution. Also he plays golf, but not well. "Ploughing the sands" is really his effort, though it has been ascribed to others. In the House he is ever alert. He never dozes, rarely leans back in the attitude of Ministerial repose. His brains are as prominent as ever.

**Mr. Thomas Rawle**
(1842–1916) Page 99
Some forty years ago a young man of the name of Rawle, modest alike in demeanour and dimensions, entered No. 1, Bedford Row, and was accommodated with a seat in the offices of Messrs. Gregory and Rowcliffes, solicitors. He has been there ever since. And now Tommy Rawle, having passed through successful stages of advancement, has attained to Senior Partnership in the firm, the Presidency of the Incorporated Law Society, and a position of no mean importance amongst the denizens of Bedford Row.

A hard-headed, astute, dominating man is Tommy Rawle. He is a fighter who throws his hat into the ring, and leaps after it with obvious delight. The solicitor with a weak point in his case need not expect concessions from him when it comes to a compromise. Yet, on occasion, the lion will roar you as gently as any suckling dove; he will roar you an't were a nightingale. For Mr. Thomas Rawle can conceal his bull-dog decision beneath a courteous affability which endears him to Judges and has otherwise found its own reward.

He is a valiant trencherman, and an annual visitor to Carlsbad, where he takes the waters. He plays golf in moderation. He never carries a walking-stick; nor does he countenance such unprofessional gew-gaws in Bedford Row. As President of the Incorporated Law Society, a post from which he now retires, he has won general commendation. He is of the stuff that would have risen, whatever profession he had chosen.

**Mr. Robert Henry Bullock-Marsham, R.H.**
(1833–1913) Page 100
"Bob" Marsham is a son of the some time Warden of Merton, for fifty-four years the most popular head of any Oxford college. He was born in 1833, when crime was less scientific and its punishment more brutal than at Bow Street to-day. He was educated at home by private tutor, afterwards entering at Merton. His efforts to obtain honours in the mathematical schools did not prevent him from finding a place in the University eleven. He was chosen for the Gentlemen in their match against the Players at Lord's, his brother, C.D. Marsham, who was, without doubt, one of the best amateur bowlers of his time, being in the same team. At four-and-twenty he began to eat his dinners at the Inner Temple.

In 1860 Robert Bullock-Marsham was called to the Bar, and joined the South-Eastern Circuit. He distinguished himself by acute discernment and sound unemotional judgement. He was never a sentimentalist to the jury, nor a humorist with the witness; but he did his work in a plain straightforward manner that won him cases.

He was appointed Magistrate at Greenwich and Woolwich in 1879. Eighteen years later he was transferred to Westminster, and from that Court in 1899 he went to Bow Street, where he now shares the magisterial duties with Sir Albert de Rutzen and Mr. E.N.F. Fenwick.

His conduct on the Bench is noteworthy for the leniency with which he deals with many of the offenders who come before him. Young men and women who have strayed from the path of honesty have received at his hands an opportunity to reform, and his kindly words of warning and advice have often had a far greater effect in checking a criminal career than would have a heavy sentence. He never displays the least sign of anger, and he favours no one. To the chagrin of many of the eminent counsel who sometimes appear before him he has made it an inflexible rule to take each case in turn as it appears on his list and in that way a prisoner is often spared the additional punishment of having to wait for trial till late in the day while the magistrate listens to a long legal argument.

The most trivial offence receives as much of his attention as the most heinous crime known to the law. He is an especial friend to the poor of his district, and is a patient listener to their tales of woe. He does not issue summonses indiscriminately, and often brings about an amicable settlement of a domestic quarrel by a kindly lecture to the person applying to him for redress, and by sending the warrant officer with a message to the person concerning whom a complaint is made.

He has read the Riot Act in Trafalgar Square. He may often be seen at Lord's. His friends have nothing but kindly words to say about him.

**Lord Robert Cecil, K.C., M.P.**
(b. 1864) Page 101
Lord Robert Cecil comes of the family that rules our country when the Radicals will let them. He enjoys the ability with which, in her constant desire to promote Britain's prosperity, Fortune has ever endowed the governing clan of which he is a member.

From Eton and Oxford—where he was President of the Union—he betook himself to London and, neglecting his hereditary vocation of politics, was called to the Bar. He was a pupil in the chambers of the President of the Probate, Divorce, and Admiralty Division, and subsequently in those of Mr. Justice Walton. Having there drunk deep of principles of commercial law, he wrote a book on the subject (with a learned friend), took chambers, and joined the South-Eastern Circuit.

However, having heard a rumour that there was a

better living to be made in the Committee Rooms than at the Royal Courts or at Quarter Sessions, he joined the Parliamentary Bar. Being clever, industrious, and extremely fluent of speech, he soon found himself largely employed in the promoting and opposing of Bills and in compensation cases; so much so that in 1899 (then being a child of thirty-five) he applied for and received a silk gown. Since then he has come to be regarded as one of the foremost advocates in that charmed circle; has represented railway companies, County Councils, and the like; and last October was briefed on behalf of the Tanjong Pagar Dock Company to meet the great Mr. Balfour Browne, K.C., in single combat at Singapore.

But heredity was too strong for Lord Robert. The voice of politics called him, and he obeyed, cutting himself off from Parliamentary practice thereby. But as he can argue a point of law he will be yet heard of again in legal spheres.

He is entirely unaffected, devoid of "side," and has many friends. He understands the mechanism of motorcars, and disapproves of Mr. Chamberlain's fiscal policy. He is known familiarly as "Bob." Some day he will be a law-officer or a Judge.

## Mr. Justice Sir Reginald More Bray
### (1842–1923) Page 102

Sir Reginald More Bray is as much entitled to judicial distinction by heredity as by his own merits. He is the lineal descendant of Sir Thomas More, the famous Chancellor of Henry VIII, and has a strong strain of legal blood in his veins. He comes of a family of long standing in Surrey—Sir Edward Bray, of Shere, was Sheriff of the county in 1539 and represented it in the two Parliaments of Bloody Mary. His great-grandfather, William Bray, of Shere, was the famous historian of Surrey and the editor of John Evelyn's Diary. Another ancestor married the sister of "Population Malthus."

For himself, it is true to say that he is one of the three best lawyers on the Bench. In his time he was the leading junior at the Bar, and the amount of work he did was prodigious. He reached his chambers at nine in the morning—he was always punctual to the minute—and left them at seven in the evening; and invariably he took work home to finish at night. In his spacious chambers at Crown Office Row he had a meagre library; just the Law Reports and two text-books—Mayne on Damages and Bullen and Leake on Pleadings. But he had a marvellous memory, and his acquaintance with case-law resembled Sam Weller's knowledge of London in being both "extensive and peculiar." His book-shelf was more interesting than his books—it was made by the present Lord Chancellor at a time when "Bob" Reid lived economically in the Temple. His chambers always swarmed with pupils—he would have ten or twelve at a time—and Mr. Rawlinson, K.C., is not the least distinguished of them. They were not allowed to smoke until after seven o'clock, but this may be explained by the fact that Reginald Bray was himself no smoker.

Few juniors ever earned so much at the bar as Bray. Indeed, I doubt whether, when he at last took silk, close upon thirty years after his Call to the Bar, he then increased his income. For many years it must have averaged £12,000 a year. He was great in insurance cases, was the favourite counsel of the Bank of England, and earned huge fees in arbitration cases. Perhaps it was not surprising that he took no interest in politics.

In his private life he has been a genial soul. He was the pupil and is still the friend of "Fat" Murphy, and they have together slain innumerable stags in the North. Shooting, indeed, is his chief relaxation, and, after this, farming his land at Shere. "Dick" Webster was from his earliest years his familiar friend, and no one welcomed him more heartily to the Bench than Lord Alverstone.

Sir Reginald Bray has just celebrated his sixty-fourth birthday, but his energy shows no sign of flagging. He has always been and still is exceptionally strong. To see him walking through the streets must be the envy of the lamplighter. And he is to-day one of the very few judges who are really liked by the Bar, for he has a pleasant manner, the great gift of judicial restraint, and an unerring instinct for sound law. His next step is into the Court of Appeal, and his destiny the House of Lords.

## Mr. Frederick Edwin Smith, M.P.
## Earl of Birkenhead
### (1872–1930) Page 103

Is a barrister and the son of a barrister, and takes his profession seriously; had a large practice in Liverpool, and since coming to London has gained a foremost place amongst junior counsel. Is an authority on International Law in East and West, and when not writing for the *Law Quarterly Review*, is composing "poems by Samuel Johnson."

Is naturally a Tory of the crusted sort; but if not shaken by opposition or struggle is reasonably clear of the lees of prejudice.

He has done much in his thirty-four years, and will do more: was educated at Birkenhead School and Wadham, Oxford: was a scholar of his college, won First Honours in the Final Law School, became Vinerian Law-Scholar, Fellow and Lecturer of Merton, and Examiner in the Final Schools. Has won, in fact, high University honours in law by dint of a good memory and strenuous industry.

In the House is already spoken of as "Single-Speech Smith," for he made his début by chaffing his opponents so wittily that the whole House was delighted with him. He has since spoken frequently, and somewhat dulled the brilliance of his first triumph. But he is certain to come again and be heard of in the future. Poems grafted on Law have promise in them, and Mr. Smith is young enough to become a great Parliamentarian.

But he is not a bookworm, certainly not a Blue-bookworm; he is, indeed, interested in all sports, is well over six feet in height, and has played football in the best company. His chief amusement is hunting, to which he is devoted.

## Mr. H. Chartres Biron
### (1863–1940) Page 104

An iron-grey head, a strong legal face, grave, yet with humour as well as acumen in the keen eyes, a brain well trained, unsophisticated by its knowledge, vigorous and lucid—here we have Mr. H. C. Biron, who, after a varied and successful career at the Bar, now dispenses justice to rich and poor, grave and gay, at Old Street Police Court.

Mr. Biron comes of an old Huguenot family settled for many generations in Ireland. Educated at Eton and at Trinity College, Cambridge, he was called to the Bar in 1886. His practice lay mainly in the criminal courts, and after being appointed successively Treasury Counsel for London and Prosecuting Counsel for the Post Office, he was appointed last year a Stipendiary Magistrate to what is probably the busiest Court in London.

His career at the Bar was not without striking episodes. That of which he is most proud is the saving of "The Heptameron" to English readers by his defence of a bookseller, prosecuted by the police for selling that fascinating, if equivocal, work. It was no easy task to persuade a typical British jury that "The Heptameron" was a book fit for general perusal; but Mr. Biron succeeded. During this trial Mr. Biron drew from the police the confession that they regarded "Tom Jones" as an immoral publication, whereupon he blandly reminded Sir Albert de Rutzen, who was on the bench, that the author of "Tom Jones" had been chief magistrate at that very court. Mr. Biron also distinguished himself in the defence of Goudie, the famous Liverpool bank-forger, and of "Colonel" Lynch, the Irish-Boer commander, who was tried for high treason.

Mr. Biron has always been a keen politician. An uncompromising Radical, he fought the Hythe Division against Sir Edward Sassoon at the last general election. It was, of course, a forlorn hope from the first, and success was out of the question, but he brought the Conservative majority down to three figures, and it is certain that no other Liberal candidate could have done so well.

Mr. Biron does not believe in surrounding his throne of justice with the awe and mystery which a judge generally regards as necessary. He considers that a magistrate should be the adviser and defender of the poor, and should make it as easy as possible for them to explain their cases. At the same time, it is his boast that no joke of his has yet been reported in the daily press.

## The Hon. Mr. Justice Charles John Darling
## Baron Darling
### (1849–1936) Page 105

Certain people are born great; others have greatness thrust upon them. Mr. Darling is one of the others. We have been in his Court on various and sundry occasions. He has reclined in his chair in pretty much the manner of any other King's Bench Judge, and the proceedings have been dull and wearisome. Occasionally my Lord would say a word—quite a simple, commonplace word. And for some reasons beyond the ken of an ordinary person, the Court straightaway rippled with laughter.

I shall not venture on the assertion that the Hon. Mr. Justice Darling is not a wit. At least two of his published works tend to prove that he does possess the divinest of faculties, but it is a faculty which, in my Lord's case, appears to express itself at the end of a pen rather than at the tip of a tongue.

On the other hand, the newspaper reporters of this world, not to mention the Junior Bar, are convinced that Mr. Justice Darling is a sort of Mr. Plowden among judges, and consequently when he opens his mouth from the bench we giggle as one man. And Mr. Justice Darling reaps the benefits in head lines of the "witty Judge" order, and the respect of the Junior Bar.

Cutting the cackle and coming to 'osses, I find that Sir Charles John Darling, Kt., is the son of Charles Darling, of Langham Hall, Essex. Born on a cold December morning in the 40's, he was called to the Bar in 1874 and took silk in 1885. He has been a Judge of the King's Bench Division of the High Court of Justice since 1897. He married Mary, daughter of Major-General Wilberforce Harris Greathed, C.B., in 1885, and no doubt as a diversion from matrimony sat in Parliament as Member for Deptford from 1888 to 1897, in which latter year, as we have seen, he was made Judge.

Mr. Justice Darling has in his time published three books, namely, "Scintillae Juris," "Meditations in the Tea Room," and "Seria Ludo." They are good, readable books, though a trifle academic, and lawyers chortle over them. Brevity and point are the chief characteristics of the contents. Some of Sir Charles' epigrams are most piquant. "Order 14 is Heaven's first law" is one of them, and perhaps the best.

But apparently Mr. Justice Darling is not writing any more; for, according to "Who's Who," his recreations now are "hunting and painting." Before the ribald smile at the "painting" they must please recollect that the Lord Chief Justice of England himself sings glees.

It is only necessary to add that Sir Charles Darling is a member of the Carlton, Athenaeum, and Burlington Fine Arts Clubs, and that he is known affectionately to his intimates by the pet name—"Darling."

## Mr. Edward Snow Fordham
### (1858–1917) Page 106

Mr. Edward Snow Fordham has graced the world for half a century and the office of Metropolitan Police Magistrate for ten years. Since his father, Mr. Edward King Fordham, of Ashwell Bury, was a Justice of the Peace, he was born with the judicial instinct deeply entwined with every fibre of his being, and very naturally betook himself to Caius College, Cambridge, to study the Law. On taking his degree of Bachelor of Arts in 1880, he married without further delay Miss Annie Carr-Jackson, daughter of the amiable and humane Fellow of the Royal College of Surgeons. Spurred to renewed effort by the joys of domesticity, he attained the degrees of M.A. and LL.M. in 1883; and in the same year, as one of the most distinguished pupils of Mr. Justice Channell, was called to the Bar. He joined the Midland Circuit, and for many years practised with acumen, industry, and success. He did not confine the exercise of his judicial mind to the practice of his profession only, but during the long, long vacation addressed himself also with energy and perseverance to becoming an authority on Local Government. A mind so judicial, however, could not remain satisfied with the mere practice of the law or a vivid interest in Local Government, and he set about collecting Justice of the Peaceships with untiring vigour. So successful has he been in the prosecution of his hobby that he is now a Justice of the Peace for the counties of Kent, Surrey, Middlesex,

London, Essex, Cambridgeshire, Hertfordshire, and Bedfordshire, and discharges the duties of Chairman of Cambridge Quarter Sessions. But his judicial spirit at last found its fullest and freest expression when in the year 1898 he was appointed Stipendiary Magistrate of North London. In the discharge of that function he has made it his perpetual practice to refrain from splitting the ribs of his flabbergasted Court by those scintillations of trenchant wit and gorgeous outbursts of old English humour which we have come to regard as the birthright of our London Stipendiaries. In spite of this strange austerity and the infrequency of his appearance in the riotous columns of the halfpenny papers, his discharge of the duties of his difficult office has been consistently marked by ability, moderation, and by what is even more valuable, humanity. When he gives the judicial side of his nature a much-needed rest, he is the complete country gentleman. He owns fifteen hundred acres; and, as an English country gentleman should, he farms them with scientific accuracy. In the autumn and winter, when he can snatch a day from the exacting duties of his Court, he shoots over them, walking up his birds in the old English fashion.

### Sir Edward Robert Pearce Edgcumbe, LL.D., D.L., J.P.

(1851–1929) Page 107

Born when the Nineteenth Century was in its lusty maturity, Sir Robert Edgcumbe, after a healthy childhood, suffered the misfortune of a neglectful private school, which so spoiled his health that he was reckoned unable to endure the inclemencies of an English Public School. Therefore it was the good fortune of the present Bishop of Durham to act as his tutor till he went to King's College, Cambridge, in the year 1870, where, in the next year, he gained the English Declamation Prize. A descendant of a sister of Sir Joshua Reynolds, and having, by a home up-bringing, enjoyed the leisure to cultivate Painting, after taking his degree at Cambridge, where he was known as "The Painter," he betook himself to the serious study of that art. He became Queen's Prize-man at South Kensington, and in 1874 won a studentship at the Royal Academy of Arts. But, unfortunately, his banker sire was afflicted with a deep distrust of Painting as a career; his obedient son turned his attention from Painting to the Law; and in 1877 he was called to the Bar. He joined the Western Circuit, received his fair share of briefs, and was appointed, in 1844, one of the first Official Examiners to the High Court of Justice. Then, at the age of thirty-three, he forsook the Law for the family pursuit of banking. But after a time he found this pursuit not to his liking; and presently retired from it with a wholesome and very lively sense of the dangers of partnership. For many years there has been a close kinship between the Law and Politics; and he entered the political arena. In 1891 and 1892 he contested South Dorset, reducing the adverse majority from 999 to 40; and in 1895 he contested Hereford City. In 1891 he was Mayor of Dorchester, in 1896 Sheriff of Cornwall. He was the first to start experimenting in Small Holdings, beginning with the well-known Rew Experiment, three miles from Dorchester, and making it his practice to sell them on the instalment system. His experiment proved so successful that many have followed, with a like success, on the lines he laid down. He is indeed the pioneer of Small Free-holds in England. Besides this labour for the common weal, he has filled almost every unpaid office in public life. He is, or has been, a Deputy-Lieutenant of a County, a Justice of the Peace, a County Councillor, a Borough Alderman, a Parish Councillor, and a Poor-Law Guardian. As High Sheriff of the Delectable Duchy he upheld the tradition of his family, which holds the record for the number of times it has held that office in Devon and Cornwall between 1498 and 1896, when he brought that number up to the round score. He has long been an active member of the Eighty Club, and has just been elected a Vice-President. Of late years he has won distinction in the City as an able chairman of company meetings. He enlivens the busy round of his life by playing golf; and he is a familiar figure at New Quay and President of the Golf Club. He has travelled much in America and South Africa, and has made the time to write several books—books so

diverse as a serious treatise on bi-metallism, works of travel, and a delightful life of his friend Arthur Hilton, the author of "The Light Green." He has a keen sense of humour, three promising sons, and many fine pictures; he is, in truth, a cultivated English gentleman who has done, and does, his whole duty by his country.

### Sir Samuel Thomas Evans, K.C., J.P.

(1859–1918) Page 108

It is now eight-and-forty years since Sir Thomas Evans was born in the town of Neath, in Glamorganshire. At the earliest possible age he betook himself to the chief school of the town and received the education there administered to him, with a stern and unbending fortitude. Indeed, he showed so striking a capacity, by his activity in winning prizes, for the imbibance of education that on the conclusion of his school career he was without delay sent to the University College of Wales at Aberystwith to continue the process. He performed all the functions of a member of a University not only with credit but also with distinction; and may be said truly to be the brightest first-fruit of the modern educational movement in Wales. On leaving this college he was articled to a solicitor; and after qualifying settled down to practice in his native district. Very soon he made his mark as a solicitor-advocate throughout the country-side, so that when he was a mere youth of thirty-one, on the death of Mr. Talbot, then the father of the House of Commons, he was elected Member for Mid-Glamorganshire, and has remained its member ever since. Soon after entering the House he decided to become a barrister, and was called to the Bar at the Middle Temple on the Tenth of June, 1891. Immediately on joining the South Wales and Chester Circuit a steady stream of briefs began to flow in to him; and its swiftly-growing volume made it plain that he was destined soon to become a leader of that Circuit. He became a leader of that Circuit, and for years held a brief in every important case in it. In 1906 he succeeded Judge Bowen Rowlandson as Recorder of Swansea. Of late he has been acquiring a large London practice; and judges of legal form were looking to him to become presently the chief rival and most able opponent of Mr. Rufus Isaacs. His appointment to the office of Solicitor-General is not only a tribute to his pre-eminent legal ability; it is also a reward of his services to the Liberal Party. The years 1895 to 1900 were very dismal years for it. There were very few real Liberals in the House. The chiefs of the Party, disheartened by the overwhelming majority of the Unionists, a majority which set the spoils of office so far beyond their reach, were playing doggedly at Achilles and sulking in their tents. But few were found to carry on the war, and of those few Mr. Lloyd-George and Sir Samuel Evans were the staunchest and most indefatigable fighters. The world, which is wondering at the appointment, and which knows but little of any lawyer who is not a London fashion, has forgotten those fights; but the leaders of the Liberal Party remember them well, and they have rewarded a man who bore the burden and heat of the day. Though his career has lain to no little degree out of the ken of the world of London, those who have watched it look for bigger things from him in the future than from many men that the world knows better. His has doubtless been a success of brains and hard work, yet it has been an easy success. He has taken every fence in his stride; and his luck has never failed him. Not unnaturally he suffers from that aloofness of attitude which comes of a sense of superiority to men for whom Fortune has not made the fight so easy, and lacks the power to appreciate the powers of others.

### Lord Bernard John Seymour Coleridge Baron Coleridge

(1851–1927) Page 109

By happy accident, Lord Coleridge is the maker of two records: he is the first peer who ever practised at the Bar, and the first English judge who has had a father and a grandfather as judges. His father, as everyone knows, brought it to Lord Chief Justice of England and a Peerage, and this Lord Chief Justice was the eldest son of his father, who for twenty-three years was himself a judge of high repute. Lord Coleridge has told the story of his family in the book

"The Story of a Devonshire House."

Naturally enough, Lord Coleridge was brought up to study law. After the usual education at Eton and Trinity College, Oxford, he became a barrister, then Member for Sheffield, 1885–94, then Bencher of Middle Temple, and at length a judge. In Parliament he was a Gladstonian Liberal, and he followed politics for a good many years zealously, but he found the law a jealous mistress, and at length gave his entire energies to it. It is Lord Coleridge's opinion that the less judges have to do with politics the better.

Lord Coleridge does not care particularly for any form of sport: without any wish to judge others, he can take no pleasure in any pastime involving cruelty, either to animals or to human beings; yet he loves the activities of the body, and finds, as he says, the open air and a field with hedges round it and here and there a tree, beautiful enough to satisfy any soul of man. He is a great walker, and as a young man went over the greater part of England and Wales with a knapsack, a stick, and a dog.

A passionate lover of nature, Lord Coleridge is a lover of high poetry, too, which he declares has been the solace and delight of all the years of his life. His home is in Devon, which he counts the fairest county in England, and he grudges the time spent away from The Chanter's House in Ottery St. Mary, to which memories of Cromwell and Fairfax still cling, and where he had gradually collected a considerable library.

As a judge it may be permitted to me to say that Lord Coleridge is already making a great reputation. He is very careful, very patient, very considerate, with a high courtesy, which is gradually making its impression, even on the barristers who practice before him, though it was, of course, at first mistaken by them for weakness.

### Mr. Edward G. Hemmerde, K.C.

(1871–1948) Page 110

Although Mr. Hemmerde is only thirty-eight years of age he already has a reputation of which an older man might boast. Needless to say, his popular success has not been along the lines he would have chosen. Most people think of him as a brilliant K.C., whereas his heart's desire is to shine as a politician. Mr. Hemmerde is a philosopher, however, and has learnt that we usually break a toe against substantial success while chasing a butterfly.

He was born in London and educated at Winchester and University College, Oxford. At Winchester, he won twenty or thirty prizes for running, jumping, and hammer-throwing, and at Oxford represented his college in Association football and at Rugby in cricket. Rowing, however, was his favourite recreation. He rowed in the University Trial Eights for three years, and captained the University College Boat Club for two years, later in 1900, he won the Diamond Sculls at Henley, defeating Howell, who had won in the two previous years.

Devotion to sport did not prevent his application to study. He won a college scholarship in 1890, a first-class in Classical Mods in 1892, graduated with honours in Classics in 1894, took honours in Jurisprudence in 1895, and the degree of B.C.L. in 1896.

In 1906 he was elected Member of Parliament for East Denbighshire, and in August, 1907, went to Jamaica, and after being called to the Bar there, won the cases against the insurance companies arising out of the famous earthquake fire. He also successfully contended the Appeal Case in Privy Council, as a result of which the companies paid about £700,000 in claims and £75,000 for costs.

In 1908 he returned and took silk at the same time as F.E. Smith, with whom he is persistently associated by the public, presumably because they differ on every point of opinion. He is now Recorder of Liverpool, while about fifteen years younger than any previous holder of the post, and his friends confidently prophesy that he will break other records.

He is an advocate of the democratic cause, a decided Free Trader, and a popular orator, who will no doubt quickly enhance his reputation when his party goes into Opposition. He has insight and decision, is a precise and logical speaker, and will not fail for lack of self assurance. He is tall and broad—and deep.

1 For more on Pellegrini, Ward, and their successors, see Roy T. Matthews and Peter Millini, *In "Vanity Fair"* (London: Scholar Press, 1982), pp. 29–36.

2 Leonard E. Naylor, *The Irrepressible Victorian: The Story of Thomas Gibson Bowles, Journalist, Parliamentarian, and Founding Editor of the Original* VANITY FAIR (London: MacDonald, 1965), p. 20.

3 The first Jehu (I Kings 16:1; II Chronicles 19:2–3) was a prophet who foretold the destruction of the then King of Israel. The second Jehu (II Kings 9:1–10, 25; II Kings 10:11) was an Israelite king who massacred the house of Ahab and Jezebel and killed many other kings and idolaters. See *Encyclopedia Judaica* (Jerusalem, 1972), vol. 9, pp. 1327–30.

4 See Matthews and Millini, *In "Vanity Fair,"* pp. 21–23.

5 Naylor, *The Irrepressible Victorian*, Supra.

6 For more on Pellegrini, see Eileen Harris, "Carlo Pellegrini, 'Man and Ape,'" *Apollo* 167 (January, 1976), pp. 53–57.

7 Leslie Ward, *Forty Years of "Spy"* (New York: Brentano's, 1915), p.109.

8 Ibid., pp. 93–94.

9 For example, Ward writes: "In those days I stalked my man and caricatured him from memory. Many men I was unable to observe closely, and I was obliged to rely upon the accuracy of my eyesight" (ibid., p. 104). And at another place Ward notes: "In the earlier days of *Vanity Fair* I was very often given subjects refused by Pellegrini. Bowles would say to him, 'Now I want you to catch So-and-so,' and Pellegrini would reply, 'I don't like 'im. Send Ward—'e can run after 'im better.' Thus it came about that I was sent off to stalk the undesirable subject because I was younger, and I was obliged of course to comply with the demands of the paper and pursue Pellegrini's uncaricaturable subjects" (p. 112).

10 In the issue of Nov. 23, 1889, drawn by PAL, i.e., Jean de Paleologue.

11 *Vanity Fair*, Nov. 23, 1889, p. 353.

12 These, and his interest in trials and in the atmosphere of the law courts, are related to the point of tedium in his autobiography. See particularly Chapter IX, "The Law," in Ward's *Forty Years of "Spy."*

13 Ward's caricatures during 1873, his first year with *Vanity Fair*, represent some of his best work. In addition to Mellor and Lush, noted here, the other four drawings appearing that year are outstanding—Henry Hawkins (p. 13), Lord Colonsay (p. 14), Edward Kenealy (p. 15), and Serjeant Parry (p. 16).

14 Ward, in *Forty Years of "Spy,"* describes the genre as follows: "The 'characteristic portrait,' although without the same qualities as the caricature, is sometimes more successful with one type of man. Nature is followed more accurately, the humour is there, if there is humour in the subject, and the work is naturally more artistic in touch and finish, and probably a better drawing in consequence" (p. 114).

15 The blandness of the portrait of H.C. Biron (p. 104) is noteworthy since Biron was Ward's good friend and had represented him in a legal matter before becoming a police magistrate. Perhaps Ward softened his art to avoid any possibility of offense.

16 Naylor, *The Irrepressible Victorian*, pp. 69–87.

17 John Arlott, "Ape, Spy, and Jehu Junior," in *Late Extra*, edited by John Milwane (London: Associated Newspapers Ltd., 1952), p. 71.

18 See, for background, M. Dorothy George, *Hogarth to Cruikshank: Social Change in Graphic Art* (New York: Viking Penguin, 1967), and J.A. Sharpe, *Crime and Law in Satirical Prints 1600–1832* (Cambridge: Chadwyck-Healey, 1986).

19 Roy T. Matthews, "Spy," *British History Illustrated*, III (June–July, 1976), pp. 56–57.

Arlott, John, "Ape, Spy, and Jehu Junior." In *Late Extra*, edited by John Milwane (London: Associated Newspapers Ltd., 1952), pp. 67–73.

Collens, Rupert, *25 Legal Luminaries from Vanity Fair* (London: Lambourn Publications, Ltd., 1990).

*Dictionary of National Biography* (London: Smith, Elden, 1908–1909, and supplements). Entries on Thomas Gibson Bowles, Carlo Pellegrini, and Leslie Ward.

Feaver, William, and Ann Gould, *Masters of Caricature . . .* (New York: Alfred A. Knopf, 1981).

Harris, Eileen, "Carlo Pellegrini, 'Man and Ape,'" *Apollo* 103, 167 (January, 1976), pp. 53–57.

Harris, Eileen, and Richard Ormond, *Vanity Fair: An Exhibition of Original Cartoons: Introduction to Catalogue* (London: National Portrait Gallery, 1976).

Longden, Alfred Appleby, *Cartoon Wit and Caricature in Britain* (London: Print Collector's Club, 1944).

Low, David, *British Cartoonists, Caricaturists, and Comic Artists* (London: William Collins, 1942).

Lynch, Boheen, *A History of Caricature* (London: Faber and Gwyer, 1926).

Matthews, Roy, "Spy," *British History Illustrated* III (June–July, 1976), pp. 50–57.

Matthews, Roy T., and Peter Mellini, *In "Vanity Fair"* (London: Scholar Press, 1982).

Naylor, Leonard E., *The Irrepressible Victorian: The Story of Thomas Gibson Bowles, Journalist, Parliamentarian, and Founder Editor of the Original* VANITY FAIR (London: MacDonald, 1965).

Savory, Jerold J., *The Vanity Fair Lithographs: An Illustrated Checklist* (New York: Garland Publishing, Inc., 1978).

Savory, Jerold J., *The Vanity Fair Gallery . . .* (New York: A.S. Barnes and Co., 1979).

Ward, Leslie, *Forty Years of "Spy"* (New York: Brentano's, 1915).

*Page numbers in **boldface** denote caricatures.*

HONORARY TITLES *are listed as appropriate*
*at time of caricature in* Vanity Fair.